MW01057288

THE
HERMETIC
SCIENCE
OF
TRANSFORMATION

THE
HERMETIC SCIENCE
OF
TRANSFORMATION

The Initiatic Path of
Natural and Divine Magic

GIULIANO KREMMERZ

Translated by Fernando Picchi
Translation of Foreword and Introduction
by Jane Rumsby

Inner Traditions
Rochester, Vermont

Inner Traditions
One Park Street
Rochester, Vermont 05767
www.InnerTraditions.com

Text stock is SFI certified

Originally published in Italian under the title *Introduzione alla Scienza Ermetica*
    by Edizioni Mediterranee, Via Flamina 109, 00196 Rome, Italy
First U.S. edition published in 2019 by Inner Traditions

Cataloging-in-Publication Data for this title is available from the Library of Congress

ISBN 978-1-62055-908-6 (print)
ISBN 978-1-62055-909-3 (ebook)

Printed and bound in the United States by Lake Book Manufacturing, Inc.
The text stock is SFI certified. The Sustainable Forestry Initiative® program
promotes sustainable forest management.

10 9 8 7 6 5 4 3 2 1

Text design and layout by Priscilla Baker
This book was typeset in Garamond Premier Pro with Futura and Fabello used as
display typefaces

Contents

Part One
INTRODUCTION TO
THE SCIENCE OF THE OCCULT

Part Two
ELEMENTS OF
NATURAL AND DIVINE MAGIC

Part Three

THE MYSTERIES OF THAUMATURGY

Translator's Foreword

By Fernando Picchi

Science and faith: the two cornerstones of modern culture and human progress. Unfortunately, these two words—or rather, the concepts and methods they represent—are too often interpreted erroneously. Thus, we frequently end up witnessing a conflict between two opponents, sometimes in bad faith, each of which tries to demonstrate its superiority over the other. This is why adjectives are applied so as to better define the two words and make distinctions between such things as blind faith and reasoned faith, official sciences and occult sciences, and so forth. It's quite natural at this point that some would include the occult sciences in the category of "faith" (an opinion that we do not share at all, because faith belongs to religion, a passive behavior, and not initiation, which is an active behavior, if we wish to limit the word *faith* to its essential meaning). Others would define some scientific manifestations as mystical or fideistic, with the resulting consequence that it becomes ever more difficult to navigate and delineate the borders between science and faith; these manifestations, as used in this presentation, should be understood, in a broad sense and as a working hypothesis, to designate a particular state of matter, at the highest degree of attenuation and endowed with intelligence, and that is customarily identified with the name of *spirit*.

A typical aspect of science as we know it today is experimentalism.

If we wish to define *science* as all that is realized through experimentation, I don't see why esotericism should be excluded from science. Esotericism has been studied and subjected to the experimental method, as I understand is the case at the various Kremmerzian Academies in Europe. The only reason for such an exclusion might be the tendency that for many centuries has driven official science (here again, we are in need of a qualifying adjective) to negate the existence of the spirit or anything that is intangible, immeasurable with its tools or its methods of inquiry, and which is, on the other hand, the underlying basis for esotericism and esoteric research. The fact that this imponderable escapes detection by certain instruments does not grant us license to affirm that such instruments or methods are the best, or the only ones that can be used.

Two fundamental truths are overlooked by all those who use this assumption to negate the existence of any imponderable. The first concerns dimensions or measurements: take, for example, the measurements that are accepted in the scientific field today—which could be totally arbitrary, because said measurements have been created and used by humans in the context of the human body and the human mind. There is nothing that proves such measurements have the same value in the whole of the universe. There could well be a dimension still unknown to us, but which nevertheless influences our world. The second great truth is that research in the esoteric and spiritual field cannot follow the same beaten path commonly accepted in the scientific field.

There are various reasons for this situation, and here I will mention just a few. First of all, today's scientific research has been made possible by the professionalism that accompanies it: researchers dedicate their lives to research and are sustained by powerful institutions that give them full-time work and salaries, because the results of their research will be commercialized and shared by humanity for its material advancement. Second, in the overwhelming majority of cases, scientific research uses instruments to observe and investigate a series of samples that are external to the researcher himself. The objective method is, in fact, the basis of scientific research. Even in those instances where the object of the research is human, it is never the researcher himself, but rather others, who will be examined. Thus, he finds himself faced with an irresolvable dilemma, which prevents every chance of complete penetration into the field of the object of research. Third, the successful researcher discovers something, which in most cases is then made available to humanity. This happens because whatever is discovered can be reproduced and provided to anyone who has the means to buy it. Regarding the accuracy of this latter point, doubts may arise for several reasons. Are we sure that all the discoveries of the researchers are known to the whole world? Do we know everything about all the weapons that have been invented so far? Have we been told everything about all the space expeditions? How many other questions can be formulated by us common mortals?

Even if research in the esoteric field starts out by rigorously following the scientific experimental method, it cannot coincide with what we've just stated above, mainly because the object of the research is always human. Often the object is the researcher himself and his relationship to the universe of which he is a part, following the Hermetic axiom that in order to understand something, one must become that something. Even when success is achieved, the esoteric researcher does not provide a commercial product, and the outcomes are therefore considered useless for humanity as a whole. The results of such research are not disclosed—this is not for the same reason as those secrets about weapons or space expeditions are not disclosed, but rather due to the skepticism, to put it mildly, with which the results would be received.

In fact, research in the esoteric or initiatic field can be carried out for a lifetime and provide great, good, or mediocre results, but these results are always subjective and cannot be objectified into a device or a box of pills readily available to everyone. Who would want to believe, but above all to repeat upon themselves, the experiment before denying its truth or classifying it as impossible solely based upon preconceptions or arrogance? Even if someone was willing to try out the experiment upon themselves and had the time to do so in their brief human lives, would the results be the same? The reply "If the scientific method is used then it can just give one result," is irrelevant and misplaced, because, whichever scientific procedures are used, in order to get equal results, equal quantities and equal qualities must be used and, as has been demonstrated by Giorgio Piccardi, that is not always true, because the same experiment conducted in Australia can provide slightly different results from the one conducted in Italy.

What then of humans? Do we respect the same premises of quantity and quality for each person? The reply is all too obvious, especially if we take into account that in objective scientific experiments the subjective intervention of humans is present to a greater or lesser degree, bringing about the nonuniformity of the results. When the principal instrument of decision, measurement, and evaluation is intelligence and human interiority, then the nonuniformity of the results is obvious given the different nature of the start or the finish, independent of the most rigid and rigorous experimentalism.

Science has always railed against dogmatism, often rightly so, an aspect to which even esotericists have expressed strong reservations, while admitting it in some cases, as the reader will have chance to discover while reading this first work of this collection. But even science has not always maintained its distance from dogma: for example, the non-transmutability of matter was, until recently, considered a scientific dogma, which is presently undergoing serious revision. The reader will be able to find many other scientific dogmas that were upheld as valid in the past and later proven wrong. Nothing can stop us from wondering if many other universally accepted scientific dogmas would not in the future be overturned, and that future may not be so far off. In fact, as Prentice Mulford stated in the nineteenth century, "it is a fatal error to look at that fragment of the past that we know and use it as an infallible guide for all that could occur in eternity."

Therefore, the two types of research—the scientific and the esoteric or initiatic—are equivalent if conducted with the same rigorous experimental method, and the one who does not accord them the same dignity and same utility simply because the results differ, is making a mistake. Moreover, the results cannot help but differ, considering what we previously stated and also considering that at the basis of each type of research there is a somewhat divergent premise or presupposition. Official science takes any kind of phenomenal aspect as law and as such repeatedly examines it; esotericism, which is here identified as Hermeticism (rejecting a priori the mystical uninformed speeches from many pseudo-initiates or self-styled esotericists), starts from the unity of the law and then sees in the phenomena the multiple manifestations or transformations deriving from that single law.

Science examines electricity and studies all the phenomena and applications as ramifications of electricity itself; esotericism, on the other hand, cannot but consider electricity as a manifestation of the single universal vibration that assumes different aspects that take the names of light, electricity, heat, magnetism, love, and so forth. Science studies human illness as it manifests itself and uses that as the basic law, which not all cases will follow with 100 percent uniformity; it attempts cure of the symptoms but does not go back, even when based on etiology, to the cause of what started the illness in the first place. Esotericism considers every human being unique, like the universe, and tries to explain the cause of the organism's dysfunction by basing examination not on the phenomenon but rather on the psychophysical unity of the person manifesting the illness. Science intervenes on the physical body to eliminate the symptom; Hermeticism maintains that intervention should take place on the human as a whole through correct use of vital force, the laws of which humans often ignore. Instead they employ vital force not for their wellness but for many other motives, which can weaken their spirit, putting them at risk of things that could otherwise have been avoided. It is also true, and undeniable, that medicine has recently moved closer to the psychosomatic concept, something that Hermeticism has always maintained and upon which various Paracelsians base their treatments. Unfortunately, they are still far from a precise view of this concept because they tend to falsify the value of the psyche, attributing to it a partial function, considering it a funnel that exclusively collects impulses that are generated by external agents. In this way, the historical ego is not taken into account, nor is the presence of our ancestors in us today, which guides the lives of each one of us without us being aware. The only concession that science manages to make to this fundamental concept of Hermeticism is by acknowledging hereditary transmission via DNA, which it has to do, and could not do otherwise, as admitting more would mean recognizing the theory of successive reincarnations. The latter Hermeticism advocates, not on a fideistic basis, but rather on the possibility of individualization of this occult nucleus in each one of us, by means of a lengthy series of experiments and a rigorous research method into the depths of the occult ego, a method not different from the scientific one, because even in the field of science intuition is frequently at the base of discovery, and experimentation follows—and does not precede—this happy intuition.

While continuing to partially maintain their positions, today the two contenders, the supporters and opponents of the physical phenomenon that we have called spirit, are slowly coming to a reconciliation. This is a tendency and a need felt and followed not only by Hermeticists but also, and above all, by broader and more open-minded scientists driven, in their research, not by preconceived ideas or dogma, but by a real desire for knowledge. Admittedly, it is only a handful of people on both fronts who have understood that it's time to abandon preestablished themes because Truth cannot be one-sided but, as has always been stated, lies somewhere in the middle. Humanity is ready to take a great leap forward, notwithstanding the strong regurgitations of obscurantism that are expressed in various ways. And it is these pioneers who must be leveraged to give everyone the answers that they seek for in vain in the current culture.

The aim of this collection is to present the writings of a pioneer to persons of good will (or who will good), in order to draw out from them, freely illuminated by their own intellect, the conclusions that their personal state of evolution will allow them to attain. To these persons, who pass through this life not to digest but to research, let all our love, esteem, and salutations flow, wishing that they be able to identify what has long been established in their heart to do, and then to bring it to a happy completion.

FERNANDO PICCHI

1981

Introduction

I n presenting to the public this organic collection of Kremmerz's writings that a group of scholars in the field of Hermeticism have compiled in order to allow the reader a concise look at some of the fundamental issues in the vast and complex body of Kremmerzian teachings, it was thought opportune to pave the way with some introductory considerations.

Parallel to the growing dissemination of scientific knowledge, which contributes, beyond current scholastic education itself, to numerous popularizing publications, to say nothing of the ever-greater impact in our lives of the technological advancements that are the direct consequence and application of discoveries in science, we are also witnessing an equally remarkable crescendo of interest in every form of knowledge that is strange, marvelous, and difficult to access—in a word: the *occult*.

There are various reasons that can explain this apparent contradiction. From a more superficial point of view, even if they contain a part of the truth, occultist—or as they are more commonly called today, "esoteric"—books, which are the object of growing interest, can be set in the framework of science fiction, or in what is called escapist fiction, both of which are widely consumed in our modern industrial societies, a fact that derives from the monotony that results from an existence organized by time. With this in mind, it certainly doesn't happen by chance that various widely published magazines promiscuously dangle, much

1

to their readers' delight, real occult topics (ancient magical practices, mystical phenomena, and so on) as well as flying saucers, the so-called UFOs, which are indeed the undisputed domain of science fiction.

If we go more deeply, however, we can sense that the interest of contemporary man for such topics often seems dictated by the need for new faiths to substitute for the traditional ones that, for one reason or another, are no longer satisfying. This is due in all likelihood to the spread of cults and beliefs, more or less institutionalized, of various merit and content, that range from the cult of aliens—the mystical paroxysm of what is called "ufology"—up to various mystical churches, Oriental or not, to some of which we must also recognize the merit of offering, at least in principle, to their followers a method to verify, by means of experience, the content of the various articles of faith.

Finally, if we wish to examine the phenomenon from a more serious and interesting point of view, we must definitely consider the possibility of directly experiencing supersensible realities. In fact, only that can lead us to the heart of the matter that concerns us—to wit: the study of Hermetic sciences.

The fact of being familiar with straightforward scientific thinking has certainly, over time, induced in the more mature and knowledgeable modern person an irrepressible requirement to take as certain and accepted only that which can be clearly known by means of direct experience. This requirement, aimed in the beginning only at the phenomena of the physical world, has also ended up being imposed upon those realities generally thought to fall exclusively to religions and that believers are asked to accept as articles of faith.

A notable indicator of this changing attitude vis-à-vis supersensible realities was the emergence of parapsychology, which offered to observe, record, and interpret, using a methodology strictly scientific, various paranormal phenomena (telepathy, telekinesis, etc.). However, parapsychology approaches the issue only from a limited point of view, insofar as the researcher in this domain remains external to the phenomenon, merely observing what is found in the prognostic or sensitive subject who is the object of the experiment, and thereby obtaining only knowledge that is indirect or mediated.

Therefore, the principles and methods of parapsychology cannot satisfy those more committed researchers who wish to test directly, for themselves, and with the same transparency with which a chemical phenomenon is tested in a laboratory, those alleged supersensible realities proposed as objects of faith by religions.

In this respect, it must be emphasized that, if we have clearly recognized this requirement, we have also noticed that it contains another, as a corollary, and that springs from the following simple deduction: if the researcher, at the level of spiritual development he finds himself, in most cases, has no direct perception of the realities he wants to know, then it becomes necessary for him to change his state in order to make possible this perception that was previously forbidden him, as is the case with a more sensitive receiver that can capture more subtle vibrations.

We thus see reappearing, because of scientific logic, the old precept of purification or catharsis, that indispensable tool needed to achieve knowledge of divine things.

Kremmerzian teaching satisfies the two postulates required for a conscious and committed spiritual search: a system of doctrines and learned practices that leads those who are qualified for such study to a direct experience of their contents. Moreover, this pronouncement, formulated here as part of such a teaching, is submitted to being personally verified by the student.

At this point, however, it is immediately appropriate to dispel some possible illusions that could, if they were not pointed out, over time lead to many bitter disappointments.

From the alleged scientific nature of Hermeticism, some could be led to suppose that we are talking about a common discipline that can be learned by simply applying oneself to it like any other branch of knowledge. Nothing could be further from the truth. Instead, one needs to realize that if the invisible world is governed by precise laws, just like the physical world, then we're dealing with laws that are qualitatively different and that can be likened to physical laws only by virtue of an analogical relationship. Said laws, however, can be deciphered and applied only in the aftermath of an active cathartic commitment that involves the entire being of the researcher, who, in addition, must already be, right from the start, possessed of a particularly enlightened and penetrating intellect.

The reader himself will see, right from the first page, the truth of what we are affirming, as he comes into contact with the difficult subject matter dealt with by Giuliano Kremmerz, to whom the credit should be given of having carried out the most significant effort of clarification and dissemination ever attempted in this field. Having formed the magisterium of this high knowledge at the end of the last century, Kremmerz actually brought about—using, wherever possible, the ideas and understanding of his time—the translation into a discursive and didactic modern parlance of the synthetic and abstruse foundations of Hermeticism, that is, of that body of sapiential data that has its roots in the ancient cultures of the eastern Mediterranean and that reached the author through a direct transmission, uninterrupted over the course of centuries.

However, every effort to clarify and disseminate such topics, and thus also including what the author accomplished, encounters a deeper limit, for these subjects open wide onto truly limitless horizons, with perspectives that do not lend themselves to closed and complete verbal formulation. There are truths that the researcher must seize for himself, training, as it were, the organs necessary to perceive them; and, consequently, the language one uses to speak of them must perforce be of things symbolic, analogical, allusive. For an example of the intrinsic difficulty of dealing with some truths of the occult, it would be like trying to explain colors to someone who was blind from birth.

You can be sure, however, that Kremmerz left nothing out that that could be expressed in plain language, placing at the disposal of the researcher the profound depths of his knowledge and facilitating, to the utmost, the intuition of Hermetic truths necessary for the researcher's evolution.

Naturally, tastes, interests, and the very mentality of today's reader have changed from those of the audience whom Kremmerz addressed, while the scientific legacy we have in our possession has been enriched enormously since his time, so that some aspects of Kremmerzian language belong to an era that is no longer ours. However, the astute reader, able to distinguish what is essential from what is ancillary, will readily see how, on the one hand, none of Kremmerz's statements are opposed to our scientific learning, while, on the other hand, his work of clarification and dissemination retains, even today, its substantial value intact, which now makes it a "classic" in its field, without however barring the path to further possible formulations.

The compilers of this present collection hope that, taking into account the necessary limits inherent in a synthetic presentation, it serves to provide the reader with a useful approach to many essential themes of the vast Kremmerzian teaching, of which, in its doctrinal and practical aspects, the Centro di Ermetismo Universale Roma is the legitimate custodian. Therefore, the present compendium could be valid as an effective introduction for those—especially younger people—who turn toward these difficult topics, leading them to an understanding that, unlike what unfortunately often happens, offers neither a false promise nor an evanescent mirage, in which case its purpose could be said to have been achieved.

An Appeal to Aspirants
to the Light*

Nothing did I know, I came in, and saw the secret things.

PAPYRUS OF NU, CANTO 116,
FIFTEENTH CENTURY BC

I

If experimental science, through its gradual conquest of nature's secrets, has made considerable progress in the last fifty years, the knowledge of the divine virtues of the human soul has, by contrast, not advanced a single step.

Today, just as before, just as always, in the light of the sun, according to ordinary aspirants to the knowledge of the mysteries of the future, there are only two categories of people: the mystics and the fake doctors who profess theories that are not within reach of all minds.

The mystics are legion: from the religious exaggeration of those who talk to God and to the saints, prophets, and archangels, right down to those who evoke the spirits of the dead.

The pseudo-doctors are those who, using the methodology of ordinary scientific experimentation, try to talk with a semblance of authority about that thing that everybody possesses and which nobody can

---

*Published in 1897.

6

explain, namely, the soul within the human creature, rich in virtues and unfathomable mysteries.

The mystics speak through psychic ecstasy, and fall under the examination of unbelieving psychiatrists—themselves mystics of an infant science—who classify them as fit for the mental ward and the subjects of experiments intended for a public that never questions the assertions of those regarded as beacons of officially recognized science.

Thanks to their linguistic games, magnetism has become hypnotism; the human mind, that is, our faculties of thought and will, has become the psyche, and under that name has become an official subject for medical experiments. But how many of them, who have a conscience, will not confess that, in this struggle against the conquest of the unknown arcana, that they are always hoping for but never arriving at any positive conclusions?

Yet the problem of the soul is always the one that is of greatest interest to the masses.

Everyone wants to know, everyone ardently longs for some knowledge of what will become of man after his death.

The mystery of death is the limit at which the study of human science as it is conceived in clinics and universities stops; but it is also the limit that Hermetic philosophy must take as its starting point to ascertain, if possible, with what tenuousness the material of the thinking ego can withdraw itself from the necessity of bodily functions.

If the skeleton is still solid, if the flesh is still young, the cells living, the tissue of the veins flexible, what need is there to go through the grave to remake oneself?

You, o Death, are the solution to the spiritual enigma within living man and within the hidden depths of his unknown soul.

The initiate must vanquish death and go beyond the slavery of the inexorable law. The initiate faces only the problem of the continuity of consciousness, the crossing of the river of forgetfulness, Lethe, continuing uninterrupted his dream of integration with divine powers.

Experimental science cannot address the problem and, in the

absence of proof accepted by science, it is content to deny that there can be any survival of the soul or of man's psychic individuality.

In this way the door to religion and mysticism is opened. Because religion and mysticism offer something that the science of the universities cannot give—the hope of a life that is free, in a world of superhuman justice and ideal liberty—it is desirable that one word unveil the truth.

But the problem of the beyond will only be resolved by those who can attain a knowledge of themselves, that is to say, of the structure, anatomy, and "chemistry" of their own souls.

I do not mean to refer here to the investigations of those who, in their books and other writings, have turned out volumes of long-winded psychology purporting to examine our predominant instincts as well as our moral virtues and how to develop them. These investigations are only preliminary researches, and this whole swarm of writers does not really aim to examine the problem of the soul in itself, but only to examine it in relation to the society in which man lives, and to the so-called morality laid down by the society of the living, considered as a condition for success in social life.

Science, from astronomy to chemistry, has brought us a great good: the repudiation of all the petty ideas of a universal God made in the image and likeness of man, and thus of the statues, pictures, and symbols embedded in popular tradition. The infinite universe, which is inaccessible to all means of scientific investigation, cannot be represented, even symbolically, as a giant man, since *man* is the product of the *earth,* and the earth is only an infinitesimal part of the infinite Universe.

The only scientific concept of God is this: *the law that governs the Universe in the most perfect equilibrium.*

This law is infinite, constant, and eternally the same everywhere: on earth, in intelligent thought, outside of earth's orbit, in the gravitation of visible worlds, in the moral displacement of souls grouped into society.

This law is perfect because it does not allow any violation whatsoever; thus, a miracle that would violate the law is impossible, and apparently it is only possible if it is the result of the law itself, for reasons as yet unknown to man.

This law is intelligent because it gives and takes away according to merit; it grants and removes with a justice that is beyond man's capabilities.

For us, there is only the Universe, with one inexorable law, with an Order from which nothing can be taken away. If you want to represent this intelligent and inexorable law in the figure of a man, I beg you not to create an idol as God supreme. The universe is too vast to be embraced in one word or in one human figure. When the ancient patriarchs of the Bible stories spoke of the inexorable figure of Yahweh (Jehovah), who bordered on cruelty and was never capricious, they in fact were making reference to this universal law that directs and creates all that exists, whose soul is *the essence of Being,* namely, the immutable primary substance and secondary and variable form.

This immutable law is also understood as the appearance of *the universal primary intelligent essence, which springs from the forms of all things, visible and invisible.*

The ancient priests of classical initiatic religions never used definite forms to represent the primary principle or the intelligent substance; rather, they always used manifold plastic forms to define different moments of the creative act, or rather, the *incarnation* of the Universal God.

The greatest conception a zoologist, a physiologist, or a botanist can have of God is to acknowledge Nature as the one and only divinity that can be discussed and studied.

Now, all the symbols and hieroglyphs of the ancient sages say this:

He has two faces: the visible one that represents his manifestation in the physical world, that is, in the Nature of our modern materialistic philosophies; and the other invisible, representing the spirit of Nature, that is, Intelligence, the law of every manifestation of Nature—a Force, an immense Soul that makes the tree blossom, shines through the water, hardens the metal, and illumines the sun.

The invisible God of the Universe, whose very manifestations are the positive proof of his existence, is the intelligence that governs all the manifestations that touch our senses.

This universal intelligence (invisible God), through the wise constancy of its manifestations, is *the regulating law of universal nature.*

The conquest of powers is no more than the right to obtain them by this law.

An athlete who trains all day long in order to be able to lift heavy weights has a right of priority over all the lazier men. A chemist who works away intelligently at the examination of natural bodies has a right of priority over all those who have never in their lives wondered what goes to make up the air. You will not be able, whatever strength you use, to bend metals, but a skilled smith, weaker in bodily strength than you, can bend them at will.

This is the right of power.

A conquest in the law, not outside the universal law.

Anyone who does not understand this is simply mad, because he thinks of power without conquest.

Is this concept, then, which is strictly scientific and philosophical, truly a modern conquest?

No one has devoted himself to the deep study of the ancient priestly sciences, other than through the symbols and hieroglyphics through which their secular secrets were passed on to us, and the priesthood of Assyro-Babylonian and Egyptian religions had no concept of God but as a law.

The priests' secret, their big secret, was the knowledge of the laws of the human soul, through which they managed to acquire marvelous powers that seemed fabulous, but were not.

Telepathy, experiments in levitation, accidental divination of things to come through dreams, premonitory signs of things that are about to occur are all things that already attract the attention of recognized science, but inconclusively, because it studies the phenomenon when it arises, like savages' knowledge of eclipses of the sun or moon:

they confirm the obscuring of the sun or moon and don't explain it, whereas, in cases of intelligent human consciousness, it is necessary:

- first, to explain the phenomenon (mediumism, telepathy, visions, premonitions); and
- second, to produce it at will.

For this knowledge of the soul to become truly and strictly scientific, it is necessary to study the laws that regulate it and the process by which it produces these phenomena.

The subjective method of conscious investigation of one's own ego, sufficient to develop its intensity and reap the rewards, always represents, without fail, the preferable method for those who ardently desire awareness, knowledge, and progress.

The goal of the integration is man.

Never lose sight of that.

Each of your experiments must be done on the man, not on any man, but on you, yourself; and furthermore, you must be conscious of every step forward and know exactly the most apt ways of bringing about a *feeling state* that is beyond ordinary experience.

II

There exists a *secret world* that men glimpse, a world whose existence they suspect, whose manifestations surprise them, but that they cannot account for.

To study it, we must first study, independently, the secret man who is hidden within us; and second, study the secret, invisible world of souls: of the dead, of divinities, and of the beings that have never been human beings and that live in another life.

The secret world [*il mondo secreto*] will have to contain the entirety of sacred science of the ancient priests, the science that turns man into a living god.

The *secret world* will be a work of gnosis to reconstruct the mysterious science of the magicians and will be dedicated to the aspirants to the *light,* that is, to those who, well balanced in their passions, pure of any harmful intent, strong of will and the will to do good, will devote themselves to study and observation in order to succeed.

The elementary parts, which serve to redress the balance of mistaken or badly understood ideas, will be set out in a way that is accessible to everyone; for the rest, I will speak in a way that reserves the knowledge only for that mental and moral aristocracy that has the right to rise.

I only promise and maintain this: that I will hide nothing, and the *Great Arcanum* will be revealed to you so that candidates for the great priesthood will find the confirmation of their aspirations.

Wordy philosophers and scientists with limited lines of research must make way for a rational school of culture that will show the way to the masses because it marks the limit where the philosopher must unite with the scientist and move toward the conquest of the truth *pro salute populi* [for the good of the people].

To be explicit, this curriculum of facts consists of the effort to better ourselves and others in the knowledge of the individuality latent in us—in applying these achievements to real life to the benefit of those less well provided for, fighting evil in whatever form of ignorance and authoritarianism it takes.

The priestly initiatic methods prepared and shaped the etheric human nuclei: the self-formation of intelligent humanity. Our school is making this attempt today. The integration of the powers is subordinated to the state of consciousness that aspires to the potency of a real and profound knowledge.

While religions proclaim that these qualities and supernatural powers proceed from the grace given by an unknown God, our school studies scientifically the laws that govern such phenomena, laws well known to certain special priesthoods, the founders of religions. It encourages the virtual powers of the living organism by bringing about, through traditional practices, self-discipline [ascesis] in the study of psychophysical powers and the development of the integrated individual, and effectively directing their Hermetic therapeutic application to mitigating human suffering. Therefore it is a school of practical philosophy whose disciples have but one aim: *to contribute to the development of human civilization, as it is conceived in materialistic form, uniting, among its factors of progress, the elements of the potentiality of the soul and the spirit in all men.*

Its Hermetic mission must be carried out against ignorance and superstition for the benefit of the masses who must be saved by means of the science of man; it is therefore an altar raised to human science and against ignorance. Working humbly and in obscurity for the good; instilling publicly and gloriously everywhere that human science will in time give complete order to human matter, that it will make peace among the peoples of the world and will fight the fear and the sting of death.

To atheists, you will say that man is king of humanity and that man's wisdom is queen of the universe.

To believers, you will explain that God manifests himself in his creations, as the tree does through its fruits.

You will teach everyone that Hermetic perfection is an admirable medicine, which the gods and high deities on Olympus brought to earth, in human guise, among suffering and ferocious men, to heal their weeping wounds and make them peaceful; that Mercury distills the essence of blooming roses and that Eros gives it to mortals if radiant Venus smiles.

GIULIANO KREMMERZ

To the Disciples of the Great Art[*]

Nice, June 1, 1917

With a deep sense of bitterness, after about twenty years, I am writing a few words of introduction to this edition of *Elementi di magia natural e divina* (Elements of Natural and Divine Magic), which my dear friends the publishers have decided to make available to friends and disciples of the Great Art.

In this book, in 1897, I began to write about these antiquated things, which nobody cares about, in a period in which it was so easy to publish a book that found no readers, and here again, twenty years later—under Cassandra's copyright—I write without hope of being believed.

I did not publish *Il Mondo Secreto* to say "I am a magician," because one gives up doing that to one's own advantage when one begins to preach to the masses.

At the time, I wished to usher in a new period in Italy in the intellectual life of the best who might read my work, by tearing them away from the empty rhetoric of Christian or Buddhist mysticism that has given us the bloody results of the present day, and to disgust them with spiritualist empiricism and the madness of talking with the dead. I

---

[*]Preface to the second edition of *Il Mondo Secreto* (The Secret World)

wanted man to understand the occult or mysterious powers, which are natural to living beings, and which are the unconscious cause of all the mystical inventions that have afflicted mankind for centuries. I wanted to show that between scientific materialism and mysticism from beyond the grave there is an unexplored realm that transforms the uncompromisingly exclusive nature of these two polar extremes, and that the science of man is located in an intermediate state between life and death, which was called *mag,* and which reveals the unknown and very powerful resources of human nature. I wanted to try out on a large scale the application of these forces to medicine, understood as the art of healing or of alleviating suffering. I wanted to go further—may God forgive me—to erect a monument to Italian Pythagorism, the source of later Templarism, and to initiate a small mental and moral reform of virtue in its practical essence in social life.

I had forgotten the calendar. . . .

I thought mankind was many centuries more advanced and, in twenty years, I have only had tastings and tests as results. Nothing concrete—except perhaps for the many troubles I created for myself by my own hands.

Now my few introductory words can be reduced to these:

That the reader understands, in reading my book, that I wanted to show researchers *not the only way to get there, but one way to intuit the existence of a secret (an arcanum)*—a physical secret (i.e., a natural secret) that very few men have known, and which now even fewer know, and which, even though it is such as to render a man more powerful than any demigod, no one can be found who sells it, and apparently it does not bring happiness to one who owns it.

The intuition of the existence of this secret is by itself enough to make laughable the mystical inventions that have enslaved men to pontiffs and divine rights, creating thereby a formalized and mendacious morality that is the cause of the great evils of the present day.

Once the old world is freed of its biblical and Buddhist legacy, and when the features and substance of any conventionalism have disappeared, then man, neither through scientific materialism nor through religions that deny any initiative, *will learn to conceive the hidden divinity of the universe* as a benevolent law of liberty in an equilibrium of justice that no human code will ever be able to sanction.

Time will be the major factor in this progress whereby all mysteries will be resolved.

Volta discovered electricity, but he did not invent it: electricity existed unknown and inaccessible, its phenomena not understood, for countless thousands of centuries.

The future discoverer of this angelic arcanum of living man will not set up limited joint-stock companies and will not market its discovery—he will be the Christ-King who will bring peace to men of good will.

But for that it will take Time, the great maker of all miracles, in order that the ideal become reality, and before this discoverer can place the legendary crown of Solomon upon his head, it is necessary that the masses undergo the hard experience of life in further centuries.

You may not believe Cassandra, but you will believe her afterward.

Do not infer that after twenty years I abide any ambiguity; I shall go further and say: take *initiations* for what they are. Two or three societies of researchers, who are *supposed* to possess this arcanum, give no more than an initiation to the neophyte.

To *initiate* means *to begin.*

Initium: beginning.

Nobody gives the ending.

Because the arcanum is of such a nature that the more closely one glimpses it, the less one can communicate about it, it can be conferred within the limits of certain powers, but never given completely. And what good is it, by the way?

Is it perhaps the arcanum of happiness, since it is the great arcanum of a power that causes fear in those who catch a glimpse of it?

But it will not be like that when Time, the great driver of new realities, will have fixed the hour at which the discovery will be harnessed by a mature humanity—and if humanity breaks the law when it is replete with good, a historic epoch will then come to an end through one of those cosmic revolutions out of which a future humanity will come to expiate the transgression in a new original sin . . . or the earth will shatter in space, and the souls, as embryonic dust, will be attracted to new lives in distant spheres. Would not any race, no matter its color, belong to humanities that have lived and completed their cycle? Extinguished, who knows, in mass suicide as a consequence of having disobeyed the law of equilibrium upon which reposes, inexorable, the phallic divinity of eternity! *Did he just call God a giant "space Dick"?*

I am speaking like a mystic Saint John the Baptist at Herod's banquets; but these are only theories without curses and without the Hebraic croaking about the apocalypse.

Drink water to avoid the intoxications of mysticism. The science of hidden faculties in the human being gives rise to madness, pride, intellectual egocentrism; think of the deceptions popping up around every corner, in front of those who presume themselves to be exceptional beings, or think they have a right to divinity.

Be modest, humble without lowering yourself, Pythagorean in the spirit of your research and in social life; I invite you to the alluring study of the exceptional. Studying is meditating and working, interpreting and testing, it is not dreaming. In the imagination—there lies the danger of fantasy, of obsession, and of bestiality.

Read the very few classics of alchemy.

Meditate.

Alchemy and *magic*—two things that have fallen into disrepute.

But it is the two words that are disreputable and not the things whose doctrine and experience they encompass: the truths that one can achieve are no more than very deep problems worthy of the interest of evolved minds that are totally free from the well-formed prejudices of the profane schools.

The alchemists have presented a problem that has not yet been solved by the official universities. The masters of the school of alchemy wait in the shadows, so that the agreeability with which they often announce their mysterious preparations gives birth to the superman who knows how to adapt the mystery for the good and for the reforming of what exists. Read those books with patience, penetrate the philological meaning of some words, in others appreciate the assonance, in still others the simplest analogy, and do not forget that in those parts that are the least prominent, among the examples borrowed from old wives' tales, some master of the art has given you the recipe ready-made. Remember that before the Grand Arcanum of the magicians there is the small natural arcanum, which is the key that even a maid might easily use.

Patient and humble men of goodwill will find the way.

Then they will find the key.

For that purpose, this book, ignored by the great multitude of graduates, will be a useful work of introduction.

I wrote it with great enthusiasm because I knew I was casting a seed that would bear fruit; I thought it would be *soon,* but it will be *later on* when a better man than I will succeed me. I also wrote it because I wanted to try out an immediate application to human medicine.

By *medicine* I mean the art of healing, of curing, and of alleviating people's suffering—medicine in the therapeutic sense. I spent the twenty years between the first and second editions of this book trying to set up a selfless human organization capable of trying a collective experiment; but I have not had the success I imagine will come later. Airplanes were not invented in an hour. The obstacles are immense; above all, the education of the people. The a priori distrust of the doctors, the sarcasm of senior officials of the state who would like to bring everything into line with an existing bureaucratic system, the religious bad faith of the believers and worshipers—all are stumbling blocks that cannot be demolished in a day.

What most people claim to want to see is the *miracle.* But even when the miracle is right in front of their eyes they do not want to admit it. This is because they want to see it as they themselves and religious fables have conceived it: as similar to stage effects in some ballets. And yet much has already been done, while doing little, against the large number of obstacles placed in front of new things and the outside efforts in designing a normal peaceful life.

The sciences of the human spirit cut through the tangled subdivisions of many branches of the science of physical man. Biology and physiology are in the vanguard; psychic experiments are part of the advance. But the problem that the science of magic and the mystery that is alchemy address is a secret that reforms and transforms a whole civilization, or a would-be historical civilization that at present makes us slaves to the corollaries of long-winded philosophies. It is a revolutionary arcanum, which is frightening to approach, because its application and its adaptations would upset all those fixed ideas upon which modern society is based.

But the first, perhaps the only, experimental side of application possible in modern society, is occult therapeutics, toward which I have directed various good friends who have followed me.

These are practicable experiments within reach of everyone, including medical doctors and those who know the ABCs of human anatomy; they can, by studying the law whose elements I set down, try the experiment.

Try, but without speaking.

Otherwise people will ask you as they asked me if you are selling imaginary powers—because people who do not reflect do not deny you and me the occult powers of a superior therapeutics, but while they deny this possibility to the *human being,* they attribute these powers with admirable compunction to a centuries-old image painted on a crumbling wall or to a worthless image carved in the trunk of a tree that has never borne fruit—without considering that the miracles from the images are the miracles of man and of the masses who adore them.

I have been told in answer several times that faith is the great heritage of the religious spirit, which can do anything.

That is a prejudice. Mysticism is a vicious legacy.

There are so many categories, and it grows everywhere like a weed.

There is a mysticism connected to all the aspects of human life, even in the family, next to the hearth or cooked in the soup.

A man who can say he is not tarred with this brush is a god among the most perfect. Magic is divine in this sense because it places the adept outside any form of mysticism and makes him the center of a magnetic field of love, the radiance of which eliminates evil, annihilates grief, and dispels suffering.

When this focusing center appears, the therapist is created. It is the radiance of love that heals, and this is a medicine that cannot be found on sale in any pharmacy and cannot be manufactured or distilled in any industrial laboratory.

In spite of all this, your music remains a forbidden sound in the confusion of songs of all kinds. Human society will stay the same until the coming of Christ the King in the style of Solomon, when love will have statues and receive offerings as there were in the ancient temples—because the ancients were the first to emerge after the disasters of the epoch when the races reached their apogee and were destroyed for having violated their own wisdom.

So I have wanted to try a therapeutic experiment—and I invite the disciples of the Art to follow the example I have set, a modest example without any mystical belief.

The new experiment will teach more than a thousand volumes could.

Do not give yourselves the object of calling ten acknowledged scientists and recalling to life a man who has been dead three days and who is stinking on account of organic decomposition.

Do not prevent a sick man from being cured by his medical doctor or from spending the little money he has on medicines.

Give yourself the object of healing *those who come to you*, without even wishing them to know you have done so, and even less without wishing them to thank you. Love them and be wise enough not to desire the impossible. Comfort them with a word and quicken in them with your love that compensating force that in human nature acts as the restorer of the vital equilibrium.

A patient who is without the equilibrium of the law of matter, with factors that cannot be determined by ordinary chemistry, without any other drug than an imponderable magnet that emanates from us, may come back, is often compelled to come back by the law of physical and psychical compensations, and works the miracle by himself. You will verify it a thousand times without pride and desire—let it suffice. Let the healing doctor be thanked and let the chemist sell his poisons. This is not your affair.

Go on studying, meditating, *without believing*—that is, beyond the faith in the things that all the world maintains.

The Myriam of therapeutists is a wave of love, which emanates from a pulsing center of unknown nature, from a man or from a chain of souls. The allegory may sound mystical, but it has a woman's name, she who was the first and the highest of the magicians, a receptacle, a deep treasure of Love, because—do not be scandalized by the truth I am about to tell—Love is matter, like heat, magnetism, light, electricity, radioactivity. Stronger than all these representatives of matter in motion, the element of Love will serve as the essential condition of movement toward the enigma of creation and destruction that the mob of mystics foolishly personifies in a *spirit* and even more foolishly depicts as a *man*. The enigma is a law.

Aim toward knowledge of it.

Whatever you do, always do good.

To do good means to love.

Love through the marvelous distance of the spheres, beyond the vision of matter that becomes corrupted and transformed. From distant worlds call back souls and the generative influences of the astral current, the Great Serpent of the Jewish Kabbalists; from the beloved soul drive out any cause of corruption by destroying the negative elements that would change it.

Consider that any nature in equilibrium, any animal organism, from the tiniest to the most advanced, tends to die because it is born with the instinct for eternal transformation through the law of love.

Love and Death are the two factors of Life. By loving you will hold off the pain of Death, beyond which the unloved soul experiences the sensual delight of regeneration through Love.

Dante repeats it in mysterious words here and there, and Leopardi sang it as in an aura of transport and desire.

You will soon understand the secret of the regenerative Myriam, as soon as you learn to love.

Only then will you be able to tell me if I have written this book inspired by the highest affection for those who read it, without judging me in advance, and with the deepest gratitude to those who, after having read it, become good, selflessly devoted solely to the cause of good, which in the future will unite men, peoples, nations as brothers and make the earth a place of love and peace.

Giuliano Kremmerz

Part One

INTRODUCTION
TO THE
SCIENCE
OF THE
OCCULT

SCIENCE IS FOR THOSE WHO CONQUER IT

What need is there today of the *occult?*

For today, what lurks in the shadows is dreadful: criminality, falsehood, deceit.

All that we know as *science* does not hide in a temple and say *I fear the light.* The knowledge of each new truth is like a stream that increases the ocean of achievements that contribute to human well-being.

Do you know something that others do not? Publish a book and explain yourself.

Thus, I have decided to write in order to make myself *understood* and to *teach* so as to help others *succeed.*

I will speak and write clearly. As for you, to understand me correctly, you should only do with scrupulous fidelity all that is necessary for you to succeed and enable you to clearly *understand* all that I write, you should *speak* as little as possible, not argue about a particular phenomenon, and not say, as the ignorant do: *I have not seen it; therefore, it is not true.*

One must study, keep silent, and wait. One must understand things well and experiment carefully. If the experiment fails, do not say: *the master is insane.* Simply say that you have not understood, and try again.

Science is every man's bread: science has been democratized to the point of making chemists of children. But men with common sense understand that, so far, neither integral nor infinitesimal calculus has become popular. And since the highest reason of occult science is the algebra of elementary philosophy, the sublime mathematics in its application to the reality of existing things, I will not be held culpable for obscurantism if minds that are unprepared for calculating do not succeed in grasping abstractions on the fly.

For my part, for those things nature permits, I will keep things down-to-earth, so that those with the least experience may easily understand; but since I also have to indicate the way to those who can see further, who are permitted to see more elevated things, I apologize if I resort to ideas that are beyond the range of shortsighted birdwatchers.

This book is written for the *many* who want to prepare themselves and for the *few* who can fully digest it.

Science is given to everyone—but only fully to the one who conquers it.

MAGIC, THE MAGICIAN, AND THE UNCOMMUNICABLE SECRET

Have you got a clear idea of *magic and the magician?*

*Magic** is absolute wisdom, which means that it is the synthesis of all that *is, was, and will be.* It is a word that covers all the attributes of divine omnipotence, if by God you mean the supreme intelligence who creates, regulates, and preserves the universe.

Magic is, as an ideally perfect science, applicable and practicable:

1. In religion (governance of collective consciences).
2. In politics (governance of national interests).
3. In families (the ethical and moral foundation of the state).
4. In man (the enigmatic Sphinx of the common learned person).

The *magician* is the one who possesses the science of God, is its living repository, and who uses it.

This science is so powerful that it causes those who have become master of the divine secret to lose any desire to speak of it; in fact, those who have reached the goal have done all they could not to write the truth except in a form that is almost unintelligible even to those who had some intuitive understanding of it.

Magheia in Greek, from which the word *magic* is derived, is an alteration of the word *mag*, which, in ancient Persian, means *highest and most wise priest*. Dr. Encausse gives this definition of magic: "Magic, considered as a science, is the knowledge of the trinitary formation in nature and man and of the way by which omniscience of the spirit and its control over the forces of nature can be reached by the individual while he is still in his body. Considered as an *art,* magic is the application of this knowledge to practice."

Just think, in fact, that ancient priests imparted this science in the temples to all those who became worthy of learning and practicing it after long and terrible trials, and it was given by degrees in rites and ceremonies that our Catholic Church has preserved in the holy orders.

Hence one can argue that those who taught this terrible science and knew its importance looked for qualities that a common man does not possess.

Just imagine for a moment that your children were to ask you for a loaded pistol, taking it for a toy: could you give them such a dangerous device without neglecting the duties of a father toward his children and of a man toward mankind? You would only give a weapon to your children on the day you are sure they will use it to save their lives, not to injure you or themselves.

The master conducted the education of the profane to its end, slowly leading the neophyte to the priesthood. The highest priest was the *adept*, that is, the one who had reached the highest wisdom: the magician.

Christ summed up all of magical preparation in "Love your neighbor as yourself." "Do unto others as you would have them do unto you." Those who practice these two precepts wholeheartedly and can keep their own counsel are ready to start.

Perfect rectitude of heart; a clear notion of what is good; a total aversion to the creation of what is bad; a great love for your fellow man; a conscience clear of any stain; no desire that is not for the good of others; no fear of the evil that may strike you while doing good; that is how the magician is like the saint and is worthy of that great idea of good that is God.

Éliphas Lévi wrote:

There is a great secret whose revelation has already destroyed a world as is proved by the religious traditions of Egypt summed up symbolically by Moses at the beginning of Genesis. This secret constitutes the science of good and evil, and the result, when it is divulged, is death. Moses symbolizes it as a tree, which is in the center of earthly Paradise, and which is close to and rooted to the tree of life, which is protected by the flaming sword, and the four forms of the biblical sphinx, the cherub of Ezekiel.

Yes, there exists a unique, universal, sempiternal dogma, as strong as supreme reason, as simple as all that is great, intelligible as all that is universal, and absolutely true, and this dogma was the father of all the others.

Yes. There exists a science that gives one powers that seem to be superhuman.*

Now, if this terrible secret exists, is it not to a saint that it should be confided?

THE UNIVERSE AND MAN IN THE OCCULT DOCTRINE

In order to understand well and clearly all that has been written on the occult sciences, magic, and so on, one must understand what lies at the basis of the theory and practice of magic.

In magic the concept of the universe is the synthesis of all that exists. All that exists is a unity, a synthesis of three essential elements: *matter, life, and energy.*

The great synthesis is completely analogous in its parts.

If you go up a mountain where no blade of grass can be found, and no birds sing, do you think you are alone? You, the stones, the air you breathe, the stars above, are all one in one universe. Take your own human reason, enlarge it into the world's reason, and you will acquire the sense of the world's reason. Your soul is the soul of the world.

From this notion astrology was born: the word (or logos) of the stars.

Hermes says in his Smaragdine Tablet that all that is above is like all that is below, and to know this is enough to work the miracle of one thing.

Dogme et Rituel de la Haute Magie (The Doctrine and Ritual of High Magic), 1854–56.

Study man and you will know the universe, study the universe and you will know man; from the universe come down to man and apply to him the laws of the universe, from man go back up to the universe and discover the occult laws there. Man has a soul, thought, a direction, a purpose: so does the universe. The universe has motion, breath, evolution, return: so does man. Everything is an analogue, and the magical process par excellence is analogy. Even the sacred symbol, which attempts are made to explain through likenesses, is analogical; so too is the law of miracles and of magic procedures, and the study of analogy leads to the knowledge of magic or the wisdom of Solomon.

The vital stream is a single one.

The process of evolution and involution of action in universal life is a constant one.

This *force* or *vital current* transforms itself according to the medium it nourishes and gives life to, and acquires a new form.

Papus wrote:

Everything is analogical; the law that governs the world also governs the life of an insect. To study the manner in which cells gather to form an organ is to study the way in which the kingdoms of nature gather to form the earth, an organ of our universe; it is the way of studying how men gather to form a family, an organ of mankind.

To study the formation of a device through its parts is analogous to learning about the formation of a world from planets and of a nation from families, or further to learning about the constitution of the universe starting from the worlds and of mankind from the nations.

Everything is analogous: knowing the secret of the cell means knowing the secret of God. The absolute is everywhere—the wholeness is indivisible in its whole and in its parts.

From what goes before, it is clear that the definition of *life*, which seems easy at first glance, is much more general than is usually thought. For mankind, life is the organ-regenerating force carried by the blood corpuscles: but this actually is *human life,* not Life. In fact, this force is only a modification of the air that includes the life of all beings on Earth. If one wants, as most contemporary scientists do, to identify the origin of life in Earth's atmosphere, one can stop there. But Earth's atmosphere, like human blood, takes its life-giving principles from above, from the Sun itself.

We can thus get back to the infinite; but since our general scientific knowledge is limited to our world, we cannot go any further, and as we realize that the force of the blood comes from the air, the force of the air from the Earth, and Earth's force from the Sun, we say that life is *transformed solar force.**

From what I have said, the analogical understanding of anything that changes in universal life becomes clear.

Let us now pass on to man, who interests us particularly.

For some, man is *matter,* for others (theologians) he is *matter* and *spirit.* For the science of magicians he is the reflection of the life of the universe and therefore tripartite in his formation: *body, plastic medium* or *astral body,* and *soul.* The *astral body* can consciously go outside the physical body, as with adepts or perfect initiates (magicians); or it can go unconsciously and consequently undergo the chance influences of the moment (wandering spirits), as is the case with any *medium.*

When the body breaks into pieces or shatters, the astral body takes flight, and man dies. If a man imposes his astral body on the astral body of another, he magnetizes him.

As I wish to set the foundations of what occultism teaches, for a clear understanding of all that I will choose and publish, I will not here go into an analytical examination of the elements that go to make up man in the formation of his astral body.

---

*[*Traité Méthodique de Sciences Occulte* (A Systematic Study of the Occult Sciences), 1891. —*Trans.*]

SPIRITUALISM

When I presented to the public, as an introduction to what we would subsequently publish, the new material, definitions, and opinions on *occult sciences,* I did not mean to write a book of spiritualist propaganda—quite the contrary. I intended to present a completely encyclopedic overview of the mystery as it is understood in *magic,* as the highest point of human and divine wisdom, the key to the occult temple of nature, in which man comes closest to God, both in his conception and in his realization.

Modern history will begin when a new type of chemistry analyzes the elements of the soul that make up the individual person and causes them to unfold, and this will mark the end of a long period of darkness in which man has not known himself.

The occult sciences include *spiritualism* as well as animal magnetism and theurgy, though spiritualism is the one and only domain, after animal magnetism, which interests those who recognize neither wisdom nor truth beyond the limits of their understanding and authority.

A French educator, Rivail, under the name of Allan Kardec, gave the first great impetus to the popularity of spiritualism, which, through successful publicity, spread everywhere that there were people who wished to talk with the soul of a dead person, or the curious who take pleasure in seeing a table move.

One could say that *magic*—a terrible word, frightful, suspicious— had been quite forgotten in the face of this fashionable success, which does not strike fearful consciences as hard as the mother of all human wisdom.

Spiritualism has been fortunate and successful because it is more suited to the common level of intelligence and closer to the doctrine of the Catholic Church Militant, because of its idealist conception of the soul, of the spirits of the dead, and of the guardian angel.

Spiritualism teaches that man is made up of three quite distinct parts:

1. The physical body.
2. The spirit.
3. The "peri-spirit," which marks the link between body and spirit.

This *peri-spirit* accompanies man's spirit after the death of the physical body.

The spirit, or human soul, tends toward never-ending improvement through successive *reincarnations*.

Between two successive incarnations, souls stay in interplanetary space and can communicate with the living. A *medium* is the person who acts as a means of communication between the spirit of the dead person, not yet reincarnated, and the living. By means of mediums the spirits can produce phenomena of all kinds: mental, sensible, and physical.

In short, the medium is a being who, because of his privileged constitution, is chosen by the spirits for their manifestations.

Those who practice Kardec's spiritualism classify mediums according to their disposition and the quality of the manifestations.

Without going into the theory of spiritualism, it is foolish not to acknowledge spiritualistic phenomena or phenomena derived from spiritualistic practices. It is certain that even those best at academic discussion and most incredulous regarding certain material and sensible phenomena have not been able to deny or confute everything. Nevertheless, the suspicion of cheating, deceit, and of bad faith should lead the teaching back to the ground of experiments that are strictly scientific and irrefutable. Recognized official science, as its knowledge progresses, rejects the old designations for forces and phenomena, and gives both new names.

The *ectenic force* of Professor Thury of Geneva is a way of being and perceiving the astral or fluidic body of the occultists—similar to the *psychic force* suggested by Cox.

So, I planned to speak of *animal magnetism*, after all I have said before to call the attention of researchers to *hypnotism*. Wise Europe, which dictates the way the scientific winds will blow, did not want to accept, as far back as the eighteenth century, the experiments of Mesmer and disputed those of du Potet, Puységur, and the others of the first half of our century, only to be then triumphantly convinced by Charcot and his Salpêtrière experiments, which gave *hypnotism* to a militant medical science, and with it a way of understanding animal magnetism.

Official science admits that in man there is a *force* (hypnotic, psychic, ectenic), but does not determine or accept the idea that this force is constantly set in motion by an *intelligence outside the active operating subject.* In effect, it admits the potentiality of this force, but excludes the mediumship; that is, it denies the intervention of an *intelligent spirit* or *intelligent entity* outside the purely physical or natural forces of the operator.

Let us then begin by not despising the occult and by admitting the existence of a *force in man that is not apparent* but is capable of increasing his potential, and let us pass from known experiments to much more complex applications, which belong to the domain of secret traditional science—*secret* for unknown reasons, but which perhaps those who today violently oppose this terrible word would keep if they realized what great effects this force can have when mastered by one who has the true key to it.

In short, then, the science of our universities, by only acknowledging the existence of a *force different from those already known,* can no longer cast in doubt this or that affirmation of occultism.

Crookes answered Balfour's criticism by saying that *electrobiological force* might have captivated him and his friends, but not the mechanical devices that had recorded the phenomena.

Well, can scientists swear that the force that fascinates, and the one that moves the control devices of the experiments, are not one and the same? And if this were the case, would not the whole edifice of mechanical experimentalism crumble?

And would it not be better to refrain from planting in weak minds an atrocious doubt that, although it is part of a very high arcanum of the secret philosophy of the magicians, I do not dare formulate for fear of doing irreparable damage?

Consider dispassionately the demonstration of facts and evidence and judge calmly, with accuracy and mathematical precision, and tell me where the experiments started by contemporary scientists can bring us.

All that has been said until now is only the introduction to fakiric magic,* the exercises of the *astral body,* as body and force, as guiding potential, active by itself, which can reach limits unsuspected by most men—but it is old hat for occultism, which the ancients knew and practiced better than us. Their initiatic schools were operating schools: at that time they did more and talked less.

But we will come back at the end of this introduction to the subject of magic beyond *forces,* in the field of *intelligences.*

• ◆ •

Let me state that the title I preferred for this work of teaching is "Introduction to the Science of the Magicians," not only because *magic* is the most proper word for synthetic science but also on account of the misuse that has been made in the contemporary world of such words as *occult, occultism, theosophy,* and so on.

I do not want to go into this misuse, and call all the attention of the reader to the worth and substance of *spiritualism.*

A true religion for the souls of the dead, as a moral doctrine, is purely and ideally Christian, with the exception of the notion of successive incarnations.

It establishes the tripartite formation of man made up of a *body,* of an envelope or second fluidic body or *peri-spirit,* and a *soul.*

It affirms the disappearance of the body at death, the continuation of the fluidic body together with the *soul.*

It states that man can develop a special sensitivity that lets the spirits

---

*Fakirs are followers of Brahmanism who use all their occult powers to produce amazing phenomena. Priests make use of them in the temples to inspire the faithful.

of the dead manifest themselves in one way or another—*mediumism*.

This, in a few words, is the whole doctrine of the spiritualists.

A table turns, a bell flies, a pen moves in a medium's hand: this is indisputable.

But how the table turns, how the bell flies, how the pen moves: this is the mystery.

The outside observer says: "It is psychical force, it is magnetism, it is radiating nervous force, it is electrobiological force, unconscious automation."

The spiritualist, on the other hand, believes that it is all the work of spirits who want to manifest themselves to men.

The ancient occult science, *the science of magicians*—of which the evocation of the dead or *necromancy* is one of the most frightening parts forbidden to neophytes—agrees with the former and not the latter. Not because the communication of a spirit with a living person cannot take place sometimes, but because generally this does not happen.

Always consider yourself as a unity under the trinitary law, like the universe, with a mental function (intelligence, spirit), a material form (body), and an activity proceeding from these factors, between the two natures, material and mental (peri-spirit). This leads to the consequence that death does not separate the physical body from an intelligent invisible body—and therefore, there are no spirits of the dead. So the real calling-up of the dead is impossible, and neither is their mental evocation in the commonly understood sense.

The mistake of the present-day propagandists for the *occult* is their rush to instill in the public at large the principle of ancient sacred science, forgetting that science (see above) is the bread of all . . . but wholly open only to those who conquer it.

The masses have religions.

Christianity, in its essence, is the religion par excellence, with which spiritualistic doctrine cannot, either as a religion or as a heresy, contend.

So what does spiritualism do?

Two things.

If it produces phenomena, it calls the attention of outside observers to the latent powers of the human organism, contributing to human progress, and accomplishes its mission because it passes from the parlors of innocent entertainment to the universities.

If, on the other hand, it does not make chairs jump and bells ring, and it seeks to bring about a conversation with a spirit that has been called up and which never gives proof of its own identity, then it accomplishes its mission of making intelligent people wonder whether there cannot be a less equivocal means of finding the truth and thus prepares neophytes for the science of the magicians.

The first mission is accomplished: without spiritualism, psychic phenomena would not be discussed today—but the second is not, because it is difficult to convince those who have gotten a taste for talking with the spirit of the Virgin Mary that they are mad.

Magic is the supreme science, the highest reason of the existing and the possible, the law of the sublime and hidden mathematics of the entire sensible universe, and the magician has to combine the purity of a saint with all the science and clairvoyance of a reasoning man.

In addition, even in the explication of the unitary doctrine, spiritualism is rudimentary.

The concept of the universe as a *unity* leads in *magic* to the principle of *unity of force and unity of matter* that some superior intellects have already glimpsed, in their studies, outside of the teaching of magic.

In this case, magic, which *no progress* of vulgar science will ever be able to find fault with, identifies many modes of existence of the one force of the one matter that begins with the metal and, from liquid to gas, passes to infinitesimal attenuations.*

Now, spiritualism admits of an indeterminate fluid outside inhabited worlds in which swim and walk many generations of spirits, covered

---

*This is the basis of alchemy, which its few researchers believe to be rudimentary chemistry, whereas it is, in fact, the philosophy of chemistry.

in their peri-spirit, who think of nothing but coming reincarnation.

This is in agreement with neither reason, which is science,* nor with the traditional dogma of the magicians, nor with religion. Therefore spiritualism is anti-scientific, anti-traditional, anti-religious.

Magic teaches instead the unity of force and of the matter in the vital or astral current—the great serpent of transformation in which, like on a very sensitive photographic plate, the smallest oscillation of a thought generates a form.†

The *peri-spirit,* according to the spiritualists, accompanies the soul of man after death and persists, while according to magic the intelligent divine principle tends to progressive attenuation, until it is assimilated in God.

This is the *nirvana* of Hinduism.

In space, where the spiritualists place the spirits of the more or less perfect dead, science places *all the fluidic forms,* all the coagulations of the fluid of universal life:

the *spirits of the dead;*
the *astral bodies* of the mediums and wandering initiates;
the *elemental spirits*‡ or spirits of the elements;
human conceptions;
the *lemures, the larvae,* and all sinful and incomplete creations.

---

*Science is light and reason.
†Astral light . . . there exists in nature a force that is more powerful than steam. A man who became master of it could change the world. This force was known to the ancients. It resides in a universal agent whose supreme law is equilibrium (Éliphas Lévi). This agent, a first manifestation of which is magnetic force, constitutes the *materia prima* of the Great Work of the initiates of the Middle Ages. It is the protoplasm of the universe, the Azoth of the alchemists, the universal pollen.
‡The French occultists, of whom Dr. Papus is the learned interpreter, use *elementary* [*élémentaire*] to mean the spirit of man after death, or better, the fluidic remains of man after the ultimate journey, and *elementals* to mean the instinctive and mortal beings between the physical and intellectual worlds. They are spirits or souls of the elements capable of good and evil according to the will that guides and dominates them.

"The astral light," says Éliphas Lévi, "is full of souls, which it liberates, in the continuous generation of beings. These souls have imperfect wills that can be subdued and put to use by more powerful wills: they then form great invisible chains and can give rise to and determine great commotions of the elements."

In the Latin forms used by the occultists of the past centuries, as is the case in our initiatic teachings in Italian, we do not use *elementary* to mean the former and *elemental* to mean the latter. Our ancient and usual word is *spirit*, from the Latin *spiritus*, breath exhaled by the creator, breath of life and love. So, while we call the former *spirits of men*, we call the latter *spirits of the elements* or *elementals*, which are creations inferior to man and more imperfect.

But this is the perfectibility or not of form and force; instead, the intelligent principles, which the ancient Kabbalah* interprets, continue the series of the progression of intelligences as far as the divine unity.

Except that this is not enough, and the spiritualists would like to know how the magician sees, how he operates, how he enters the astral realm.†

First of all, it is by reasoning. Reason is the first torch that brings us closer to truth. Second, by not deluding oneself. Finally, by forcing oneself not to speak, being without any pride, and without "casting pearls before swine."

IN CONCLUSION

They have mouths, but they speak not:
eyes have they, but they see not:
They have ears, but they hear not:

---

*The Kabbalists are the occultists of the Western Jewish tradition; the foundation of their philosophy is the Kabbalah, the framework of absolute ideas in nature, the teaching of which was traditional from master to disciple.

†Curious phrases that suggest that those who use them get entangled in a thousand inaccuracies, even of rudimentary ideas concerning magical practice.

noses have they, but they smell not:
They have hands, but they handle not:
feet have they, but they walk not.

PSALM 115

Dearest Friends,

In this didactic introduction I have put together in logical order the complex of definitions, opinions, and teachings that can better help the understanding of all, and that I will publish in this anthology.

Summing up, I have wanted to make a clear distinction between two things that the mob mixes up:

1. The pseudo-intelligent physical phenomena that the human organism (soul and peri-spirit) can produce under certain conditions of the nervous system: this is called *spiritualism*.

2. Absolute, universal wisdom, the key to all sciences—which no human progress will ever find fault with—absolute wisdom, which has the key to all that exists, which tends to develop the *divine faculties in man, and which links him with the gods, who are neither spirits of the dead nor miscarriages of terrestrial life, nor elements of the universal life:* this is called *magic*.

Logically, magic includes spiritualism, magnetism, astrology, alchemy, and all the known varieties of the manifestations of the occult forces in man and matter; but at the same time magic includes a higher philosophy and an occult philosophic practice, which gives the jumping-off point, for those who understand it best and can master it, to leave the world of the phenomena of matter and enter the world of *divine Unity*.

In this second aspect, *magic* is divine wisdom, and the magician who has attained it no longer belongs to this world of suffering and illusions, and as long as very arcane reasons make him walk in the human mud, only his physical body belongs to the earth; his Self, his intelligent individuality lives in that heaven of sublime truth, to which Dante and the Neoplatonists of his time alluded in the symbolism of Light, preparing himself, praying and waiting to be *God*.

Part Two

ELEMENTS

OF

NATURAL

AND

DIVINE MAGIC

*Unus, Pollentissimus Omnium!**

O Sun, radiant God, our father, you who create forms and give through shade relief to visible things in the wave of your eternal splendor, illuminate with your *divine light* the one who, pure of mind and heart, reads in this book the laws and practices to rise to the power of the gods: let him understand and not misunderstand; give him the humility of knowing he is ignorant and the virtue to rise above the visibility of earthly life so that where the voice of the Beast seduces him not, he may feel the breath of your fertile Spirit.

O Sun, you who sweep the darkness of the great night of passionate phantoms, of the ghosts of the most uncontrolled desires, of the proud creations of human arrogance, illumine the ignorance of the one who, purged of the influences of the voluptuousness of temporal things, is thirsty for the eternal truths—and let the idolater of the Beast, bound to the vainglory of ignorance, feel your divine ray and prepare himself for the advent of Christ.

O Sun, shining God, forgive those who read me in bad faith, quackish or blind priests, the doctors of theology who cannot make out the word of your Spirit, learned adorers of carbolic acid, of microbes, of serums, the critics who do not know, the bigots who are afraid; let your Messengers of Light, winged angels and horned demons convert them to the understanding of the truth of invisible things.

But you who hide your light only from the blind, *O Sun,* do not deny your ray and providence to the one who, reading without virtue of soul and heart, wants one single proof to be converted to truth. But if the *proof* is not enough and the tempter of the gods obstinately makes another attempt without faith, be as clement as you are magnificent.

Forgive the frailty of the presumptuous. Let not your red fiend excite his blood, and let not his brain erupt with madness at the wandering, fleeting images of lust for the nonexistent.

Forgive, *O Sun,* and check your terrible anger against ill-intentioned

---

*[One, strongest of all! —*Ed.*]

sophists and the minstrels of human wisdom. While they deny, the cock crows, and the dawn of the light of the souls, of the intelligences, breaks in the east, above the very high mountain peaks which hide the city of God from the human eye.

While they mock what they cannot see they caress the sheep, which are about to be sheared, and the fat thrushes, which are about to be plucked, look for the paper money and the paradise of the slums—meantime the cock crows again, dawn becomes sunrise, the world awakens to the light and leaves the owls, mistresses of the long night, in their nests to peck at the corpse of the great lie that fed them last evening.

To those who believe, who love, who hope, goes the true sense of my word, which is your law.

PREPARATION

I

If, after reading the introduction in which I have condensed, with broad strokes, all that has been said and written on this problem of the incredible, you have decided to continue reading what I promised, I warn you that from now on I believe I have the right to consider you my disciple. And as my disciple I warn you that if you want to enter the world, which the others cannot find, you must not believe illusions, the prejudices of your vulgar conscience, and though the nice profane paintings are seductive in their variety of colors, prepare to see around you the illusions of habits *disappear* and to see where the others only find the blackness of darkness.

The effort of all human intelligence is toward grasping the secret of God, and hence the hotchpotch of profane sciences from astronomy to analytic chemistry, from meteor physics to speculations on microbes, from experimental physics to the physiology of the nervous system, and from embryological sciences to all other sciences, infinite in number, which, newborn or about to be born, seem to be the last word of truth, while they are in effect no more than suspension points in the blindness of the great human mass attempting to climb Olympus.

So, since time began, humanity has been divided into two distinct classes: the *simple,* who, unaware, recall the *world before human malice,* and the *cunning,* who deny everything so as not to be classified among the fools. The former have *faith* as a companion; the latter, *fear* of being deceived: they are the extremes whose mean term is represented by the *enlightened* ones who were and are always present in all countries, all races, all times, to act in the darkness of the human journey as a torch for the wave of creatures who amid vainglory, spasms, and impotence are on their way to fill the cemeteries full of bones, where vanity erects mausoleums that seem eternal and are in the view of eternity only a flash of light!

The seers, the enlightened, the initiates of all times have preached and preached that, if the mob of the imperfect is allowed the sweet hope of faith, doctors are not allowed to pretend to be Christ's judges, wanting to treat divine manifestations with the same method Galvani used to deal with frogs. And in this work, once more, I warn these false men of wisdom, whose genius has been diverted by profane doctrines, that the knowledge of Jove cannot be considered as a toy and an object of human vanity.

Hermes, in the ancient magic aphorisms, patrimony of eternal divine revelation, teaches that to be familiar with a dog it is necessary to change oneself into a dog, an aphorism or mysterious dogma that must be interpreted literally: you will become a god, an angel, a demon or devil if you seek the friendship of gods, angels, or devils, and in order to have a relationship with the souls of the dead, you need to live the life of the dead.

In this lies all the practice and doctrine necessary to enter the invisible. Those who do not have the courage to abandon their worldly illusions and put intellect above all fleeting and deluding sensations of matter; those who, even if they declare themselves strong men with very pure hearts, cannot master the pleasure and pain of human nature—

they must renounce the world in which the purest and most perfect beings have the understanding of truth.

The ancient schools of initiation, from the Chaldeans to the Egyptians, and from the latter to the Templars and their heirs, did not accept a disciple without testing his courage and faith. I mean trial by fire, resistance to the temptation of desire, the courage not to quail before frightful apparitions.

I am sure you would win the prize despite everything that was the nightmare of the priests in days of old. But there is a monster you must defeat before you knock at the door of the occult. This ogre of conscious youth is called *public opinion.* You are not afraid of monsters, of fire, of the elements, but you, as a result of the false social upbringing of our times, may be afraid of *what people will think of you* if they find you with your nose in a "madhouse" book, or indulging in madmen's habits!

That is the fatal moment.

If you are insensible to the scorn of the mob, if between the well-defined equilibrium of reason and the words of the people who mock you, you are strong enough to separate yourself from the world, you will begin *to be:* you begin *to live your own life;* you begin the victory over the numerical majority of illusions, and you will see that the picture changes as soon as your genius touches your forehead and shows the mob that you are superior to vulgar nature. You will see the people who mocked and laughed at you come and ask you for a response or a prescription to avoid a catastrophe.*

The only check on the actions of the disciple must be the reason of freedom, the balanced judgment that gives the intuition of the perfectibility of the human spirit.

---

*After the opinion of the mob you might be cooled down by the doubt that your Christian conscience may not clash with the studies that you have freely started. I assure you I will always keep in harmony with the Christian authors who have written about these things of ours, and which the Church of Rome has neither excommunicated nor proscribed: I refer to Johannes Trithemius, Benedictine, abbot of Wurzburg; the Jesuit father Kircher; Raymond Lully; that sublime doctor Saint Thomas Aquinas, and others who will be very suitable to illustrate my argument.

The brain of man is a sanctuary that reflects in absolute logic all the splendor of divine reason when it is not shaken by the congestion of human passions.

The abbot Trithemius in his *Steganographia* gives the prescription necessary in order to enter into the occult. *One must be endowed with all the virtues, have a clear conscience, desire good in the name of God, for oneself and others; one must not tend toward base things or actions.*

Good attracts good both in the visible and in the invisible world. In human society affinities of character, of culture, of education, of tendencies, and of passion bring men together in groups. In the invisible world the same law applies. At the level of intellectual synthesis, all men are equal, just as all flowers are flowers, but a chrysanthemum is not a poppy and a white lily is not a red rose. There are men who are gods and others who are beasts. Civilization makes them brothers because the divine law aims toward the redemption of lower natures, the evolution of matter and souls toward Eternal Light.

Even we, who practice most fully love toward our neighbors, do not approach people we find repugnant.

Therefore, all the preparations for priesthood of all times have the same prescription, and Christianity goes hand in hand with operant magic.

Darmesteter* mentions the *asha* of the Parsis, *so dear to Ormazd [Ahura Mazda], indeed characteristic of the divine world.* The *asha* for the Parsi is purity and contains three elements: good thoughts, good deeds, good words.

I call your attention to one thing that has to be clarified: the difference between *religion* and *magic,* between *saint* and *magician.*

Religion is the entirety of a whole sacred doctrine, fit to be understood by the masses: if it has a true, deep, scientific origin it speaks to the mob under the guise of divine precepts and admonitions. It personifies divinity and speaks a relative morality to the progress of the masses.

---

*Darmesteter, *Ormazd et Ahriman* (Paris, 1877).

Magic, wisdom and teaching about what exists, the synthesis of the laws of created things, the process of creation itself in the order of truth and nature, is the key to all the traditional religions.

Both the religious man and the disciple of *magic* look for knowledge of the divine world; the former *passively* by applying religious precepts, the latter *actively* by trying to force human nature and enter into the invisible world, to discover the laws and use them as masters would for the conquest of divine powers.

The religious man may become a *saint.*

The disciple of magic must either become a *magician* or disappear.

Sanctity is a virtue of the initiate, not his purpose. The *magician's* purpose is divine integrity with its superhuman virtues. The *saint* may come to grace; the *magician* must accomplish divine actions.

The former does not need science; the latter cannot exist without science.

A pious friar, after a long life of self-denial and prayer, rejoices in the stigmata of the Crucifixion. A scientist must be able to explain that which is the cause of these stigmata.

The pious friar has no desire, he is at the mercy of God's grace and is made an instrument of it: he heals the sick, predicts a joy; he comes to the aid of the needy when he is least expected.

The *magician,* according to his powers, must give and perform whenever he wants to and whenever he has to use his wisdom, his power, the forces at his disposal.

Sanctity is obtained; *magic* is conquered.

Chaignet in his study on Pythagorean philosophy says: "All the rules of Pythagorean life can be summed up in this great maxim: first become a man, then a god, unite yourself in close relationship with God, follow and imitate God." But this did not refer only to Pythagorism. The neophyte of the earliest Christian rites wore white as a sign of "candor" (in the original sense of the Latin *candidus,* from which *candidate* derives), and white vestments are still worn by the Christian priest celebrating the Mass, but they have become *shorter* in the surplice worn for minor services, because the character of divine science is white, like the color of the moon, which is under the feet of the Immaculate Virgin.

But, my dear disciple, let us not plunge into symbols, which the *great men* of today describe as the first sign of decadence. Let us go back to where we started: if you break with the common people, you knock on the door of the invisible.

Whom do you invoke or evoke? A god, like the theosophists; a genie, like the Kabbalists; an angel, like the Christians; the souls of the dead, like the spiritualists?

Intelligent beings are divided into three classes: the *gods,* who are above, too far above for a common man to understand or perceive; the messengers of these gods, *daimons* or *angels,* who are in contact with us; and *men.*

"Be confident and courageous," said the Pythagoreans, "because man belongs to the race of gods." He is not a dethroned king, but a king in exile, who is waiting for and slowly working toward his return to the throne. He is a splendid bird whose passion for pecking in the mud has pinned his wings, covering them with clay.

The Pythagoreans warned:

Purify your body and your soul. Let reason be the sovereign and absolute guide of your life, and at the moment when death releases your soul imprisoned in your body you will become a god.

Genesis 3:22 is translated from Hebrew: *"Ecce Adam quasi unus ex nobis factus est, sciens bonum et malum";* which Monsignor Martini translated having God say: "Now Adam has become one of us, knowing good and evil," and then he comments the *us* refers to the three divine personages, while the occult meaning is that Adam was created like unto the gods or the *spirits of God.*

Therefore, I consider my disciple capable of showing all his divine qualities, far from the vermin who pontificate slowly and incredulously, and of being above the infantile pleasure of hearing the applause or jeers of the sheeplike followers of science. I want him to be capable of perceiving the beauty of this man-god, who still in his cloak of skin and muscles aspires to a perfection, which is not denied to other men, but which other men deny themselves for the vainglory of being like all the others.

You, my disciple, by escaping from the common herd, come nearer to the gods; let the faithful pray in churches, synagogues, and mosques; let peaceful creatures tickle their fancies with tables that rattle, or rise up; enjoy the fact that curious and presumptuous scientists give their opinions on the *physical effects of mediumism;* rejoice that they work for the sake of humanity and its progress, because the whole encyclopedia of phenomena comes down to putting a sensist and gross materialism on trial and to building an altar to the *spirit of man.*

Dear reader, I forbid you, in my duty as a master, the freedom to use your common logic in regard to what is related to your spirit, which is not common, and I tell you that the day you place your faith in the reason of one man you will forever give up your own, which must be modeled on and perfected by universal reason, which is in line with your divine nature.

II

The second part of the preparation for magic tends to instruct you, through outlines, where to begin in order to succeed, how to place yourself outside doctrinaire soliloquizing, and how to see and touch and learn through your own experience and not through the experience of others.

If, in carrying out the first part of your preparation, you are courageous and good in the widest sense of these words, if you understand precisely that *your spirit,* in its cloak of flesh and blood, is susceptible to all improvements to the point of becoming like a god of Olympus, a major deity, you can wait and enter into relationship with natures that are higher than the gods in the heavens.

What are these middle-range divinities, these creatures or daimons or angels or messengers of God, with whom you will come into contact? Or, better, of what nature are these intermediate gods whom you must deeply wish to know?

The best treatises on occult sciences tell you that, beyond human nature, in the *ether,* or in the *astral light region,* there exist the spirits of the dead, the astral bodies of the mediums and initiates, the elemental spirits, the human conceptions, the lemures, the larvae, and all sinful and incomplete creations, as I covered in the introduction. But according to the first precept of the foregoing preparation, you must *think and reason for yourself.* The initiator says to you, "Don't believe." Between faith and science there is an abyss. The initiator does not say "Believe"; he says "Experiment."

Now you must form for yourself a concrete but general concept of *intra-divine natures or daimons* in their plastic forms as the ancients did, without clear-cut details that are more or less stupefying.

It is sufficient for the student to have a general idea of what he will meet, and I follow the ancient method.

So will you.

Gods, daimons, and men—among them the same relationship exists as among the three states of perceptible matter: that which is heavy, that which is light, and that which is evanescent. The synthesis of nature presents the *three states* of matter: solid, liquid, and gaseous.

This number three recurs in the kingdoms of visible nature. This number makes up the series in divine progression: *man* (the heavy body that imprisons an intelligence), *daimon* (the light body that comes near to intelligence), *spirit* (the evanescent body, which has not even an ideal form, and is symbolized by light).

The philosophers say the theology of the ancients was symbolic; that the individual *daimon or genius* represents conscience, the sense of reason of a being.

All right. That is one side of the question.

But sacred wisdom, which the ancients manifested in their esoteric expositions, had three sides:

(a) a common side, which was used for the profane;

(b) a symbolic side, which was philosophical;

(c) an arcane side, which was sacred and reserved for those who had the right to enter the temple.

What is the *daimon or genius* as defined in the plastic form of pagan esotericism?

The ordinary man today would only smile. The daimon of the ancients and the protective genius of the Platonists are the putative fathers of the *guardian angels* of Christianity, and they are poetical figures.

Those who make a show of their doctrine are content to see in the *daimon or genius* the soul of man in its essence as reason and conscience.

Those who, on the other hand, are conversant with the sacred terminology of the philosopher-priests, and have the key to the three sides of the arcane idiom, know that the third, true, profound meaning of the *daimon or genius* of the ancients corresponds to a ray of light of what is: a truth that is the first toward which you, my disciple, must aim.

I will set you a problem to solve: in order to succeed, you have to study and practice the *scientific* theorems that magic teaches you or to which it alludes. You will understand their essence by studying and practicing. If you practice without reflecting, you will become an ignorant experimenter.

The first goal you must place before your eyes in your approach toward the occult domain of the spiritual nature is to attempt to know the *spirit* or *daimon* or *genius,* which represents the step immediately above your nature as a more or less perfect man. The Christian angel is a spirit of absolute purity and a messenger of God—the daimon, on the other hand, can vary in its tendency and purification.

I will use the term *genius* to escape from restrictions and definitions. Once you have started to know your own genius, you will be able to define the first . . . and when you have known many, you will be able to have an approximate, but still imperfect, concept of the golden ladder, which starts from the least pure and ends with the most perfect.

What should you do in order to know your own *genius?*

The ancients taught that to know it one had to propitiate it by practicing justice, by the innocence of our habits; then it will help you with its foresight in the things you do not know, give its advice in your moments of indecision, come to your aid when in danger, and it will not deprive you of its assistance in adversity: at times in your dreams, at times in visible signs; at times by appearing to you, it will help you to avoid evils. It will bring good upon you, it will raise you when you fall, it will sustain you when in doubt, it will lighten the darkness of your research, it will keep your fortune good, holding off bad fortune.

What will your master tell you, so as not to resort to Christian mysticism and the veneration of pagan cults? Only one thing: "Be a man, be reasonable, and dominate with the continuous mastery of your judgments all the illusions of the gross material senses of man; develop in yourself the consciousness of being, and if you deserve it or if you force outside nature, into your consciousness will come Raphael or Astaroth—the angel or daimon—your genius will certainly appear," and like Dante you will have found your Virgil, and with Virgil the nonstop train to either the madhouse or divine wisdom.

At this point, the disciple interrupts me:

If these daimons are not visible because their body has no material that is visible to our eyes, how can I come into contact with them? I will not see them, hear them, or feel them down here. . . .

That is clear.

You have to form a clear concept for yourself of what, in its true significance, *astral light* is.

In Greek grammar the word *aster* means "star." In hieratic Greek, *astron* is made up of the negative prefix *a-* and *stereon,* the state of being fixed or solid, and thus means without fixity, wandering, and therefore *astral light* in its secret sense is the light that is not fixed, which is wandering, ethereal, evanescent.*

Close your eyes, call up an image and observe it. In the darkness of your self-induced blindness you will see with a kind of sight, which although it is within all men's reach, is not the ordinary capacity to see, as among other men.

In this way, by a very simple action, which every man can do, you will begin to set in motion an exercise, which, if you just carry it on a little, will give you the idea of an *ethereal light* that is quite different from the light of the ordinary kind of sight. When you sleep and dream, the images you see are lit. And yet there is no sun, and that light is not sunlight or electric light; it is *ethereal or astral light*.

The latest writers have called it the unconscious, but in Hermetic and magic terminology it is the *astral field* or the dark field, the source and repository of all our consciousness, but of this source and repository we have no awareness except the recollections we draw from it through continual evocations by means of memory. The astral, dark, mysterious field, which is within ourselves, that is in every human being, exists also in the immense synthesis of the universe. In a man it is the occult repository of his history; in the universe it is the matrix of all the lives that have been lived, of all the forms that have been imagined, of all the thoughts that have been willed. The universal astral field or current contains in itself all the partial astral fields of all men. Therefore, from one's own astral field one can penetrate the universal astral field and from this come down to each of the particular astral fields.

We said earlier that we men are concrete individualities in matter, living analogously with the universe; that is, individualities in an analogical relationship with the larger universe.

As in men, so in the universe; if it is analogical to man, there must

---

*The tunnels of Orpheus and the subterranean or priestly cities of the ancient initiates were astral, that is, without sunlight; and there the neophytes began to learn the truths; therefore, we often find the ancients speaking of the stars, and instead of looking in the sky, we must look below ground.

be a kind of colloidal repository, invisible and imperceptible to us, where all the concrete ideas, the passions and actions of men, nations, and peoples are recorded and contained.

This invisible part of the world containing this form of invisible but easily sensitized matter is what is called the astral region.

When you say "if you recall" of a person you have seen, you are searching in your unconscious for the image of the person that you have seen and are evoking.

But when you say, for instance, that you want to evoke the image of Dante walking the streets in Ravenna, you might have seen a portrait of Dante, but your unconscious will not be able to give you the image you require. Then you invoke the image of Dante Alighieri, and if you believe in spiritualism you think you are invoking the spirit of Dante by the form he takes. Whereas your unconscious, if it is very sensitive, must tap into the universal unconscious, where Dante Alighieri's image has left its mark.

So the astral region is a dark region, which is within ourselves, in which everything that is thought, heard, and everything that comes from the experience of our senses is recorded.

Astral force is a synonym for the force of the subconscious, aura of the unconscious.

From this interior region, which records every perception, every thought, and every feeling, on certain occasions a change emerges, owing to which one feels the manifestation of a force that is released.

Anything that is released from us and represents an effort or a great impression is fixed first on our unconscious as an individual and then in its complex and synthetic phases it is fixed on the universal collodion.

Since there are an astral region and an astral force, there must be astral matter.

You cannot conceive of an occult force and matter unless you get sensory material proof of this movement or this matter. Therefore, when you hear true magicians and not storytellers of magic speak of an *astral current,* you should not think it is the fluidic current coming from the stars but the vibration of the *ether* of the Orphic initiates, that is, the manifestation of the perpetual vibratory motion that pagan theogony deified in *Mercury,* the eternal generating motion of all the arcane phenomena of mental light.

At Mercury's temples and feet there were wings; in his hand his caduceus, the rod with two serpents making love, an active and a passive current around a projector of fluid. So the caduceus has become the symbol of chemists because health, in occult medicine, is represented by two currents of ethereal fluid in equilibrium around a projecting instrument, an organ symbolized by a rod, from which you will later see how the magician's wand came to be, what use it has, and what mysteries it conceals.

Now, as soon as you have formed an approximate idea of an *interior light,* you will be able to pass from the known to the unknown without being too much of a sophist.

Get three or four or more people to close their outer eyes in the same way and open their intellectual or inner eyes to the perception of this world, which is glimpsed at first, and then seen with a sense that is a synthesis of the other five; you will then have established by this *relationship* the communion of the light that each of the observers has perceived.

I beg you to reread and understand well the last paragraph if you have not understood it properly, because I cannot find more exact words in human language to indicate a phenomenon that, although it is within every man's power, is not observed by those who do not concentrate and do not spiritualize themselves in order to do so.

The relationship between the astral vibrations perceived by the observers makes up the astral current that, in due time, you must learn to master.

Now, silence in religious communities tends to diminish as far as possible the action of all that can disturb the spirit or impede its development—so that the physical arm of the monk finds the arm of Christ!

This *astral current* is symbolized by the serpent in the Bible as it winds round the tree of good and evil, which means that the two aspects of the serpent are the low, earthly, or muddy one, which generates illusions, that is, lies, while the upper part is truth and light.

In mythology Apollo pierces with his arrow the serpent Python, born out of the slime of the earth; nevertheless the Pythian priestesses (those who had the spirit of Python in their bodies) gave responses and prophesied. Giuseppe Balsamo, the well-known Count of Cagliostro, whose name, to fools, evokes that of an impostor, but who in the eighteenth century was called "the Divine," had as his symbol a serpent pierced by an arrow, that is, the astral current pierced by a powerful and mastered will. This serpent is at the feet of the Immaculate Virgin because virginity and purity condemn it to immobility and dominate it totally. But when you don't model yourselves on the divine Apollo, or on Cagliostro's willpower, or on the superhuman virtue of an Immaculate Conception, the serpent will entwine you in his coils, dominate you, and kill you fluidically.

III

The preparation for magic is as follows:

(a) To possess unlimited courage, and cold reason that is not kindled at the first flash of illusion.

(b) To have a high sense of rectitude and morality, and to be afraid in their name of abusing what one tries to snatch from the unknown.

(c) To wish for light, in order to comfort those whose earthly imperfection prevents them from seeing.

(d) To understand and make it understood that man has within him all that is necessary to develop the superhuman qualities of his spirit.

(e) To be persuaded that upright consciences, desirous of good, and being reasonable and whole, without hypocrisy and fear, invite the genius who is closest to the nature of the individual to become manifest.

(f) To be persuaded that the tide of opinions and trite phrases misrepresents, twists, and renders badly the language that the genius addresses to our conscience, and that we close our ears to truth in order to listen to lies.

(g) To be persuaded that if the *genius* is taken as a guide, the astral serpent that appears as a sign of the struggle is dominated and one becomes a god; if, instead of understanding, one misunderstands, or rather one dreams of reproach, then one falls into the serpent's mouth.

It is the moment to say a few words on the *occult* and the *mysterious* related to the duty of the aspiring magician to *keep silent.*

Little by little, as the investigations of the learned progress in the determination of the latent faculties of the human *materia,* they come across new and unsuspected properties of our organism, and not only are the unheard-of wonders of the human body discovered but radical changes are glimpsed even in the definitions of *our* physics and *our* chemistry, at which the researchers of the next century will laugh, considering them as very flawed things.

The silence of the surroundings for the spirit is almost like abstinence from indigestible foods for the stomach.

But we must further distinguish outside sensations from sensations through *repercussions,* about which phenomena a treatise on the mathematics of sense might be written.

Your neighbor speaks to you. His *words* awaken a sensation in you. But if you pronounce one word, the work is doubled, because you must *conceive the idea, put it into words, and project it in the spirit* of that one listening to you. The word you pronounce is a *fluidic projection of your conception,* and the proof of this intensive effort can be found by any observer who, when hearing a word that does not correspond to an *already-held* idea, must mechanically concentrate in order to catch the *fluidic conception* that accompanies the projected idea.

In magic the word is an instrument of realization, and *silence about the sacred things of Truth is the way of keeping pure, and for giving more life to the ideas that should be projected, while preventing the repercussions of projected ideas from upsetting the means of reception of the magician.*

In order to escape from the quagmire of concepts ingrained by profane education, in order to purify himself of all the living or impure images with which we are pervaded in our impure life, in order to drive out of our minds the great mass of impressions of human error, the disciple of magic will make endless efforts and long sacrifices; once purification is reached, intellectual perceptions come. They are indistinct and then fleeting flashes, and later clear ideas. If by using human words you want to define the fleeting glimmer of the first light, you will be wasting your time; if you make your *perception* concrete and project it with your words, you will have betrayed its nature; you will have tried to make human what is superhuman and divine, which reveals itself only to the best and, like a sacrilegious man, you will lose the reason of that light!

As regards the question: Does magic really have a terrible secret that should be kept and hidden? And would the revelation of this secret, the *arcanum of all arcana,* be such as to destroy a world? I will answer in a few words:

The philosopher glimpses a truth, which he cannot grasp, the secret of life, of death, of the reason for being, of the end of men, nations, races, and species. The Sphinx is the symbol of this problem. The disciple of magic must set himself the aim first of arriving in the presence of the last monster, which foreshadows the final problem, and then of dominating it, which is what Oedipus failed to do. If the magician succeeds in riding the monster instead of cutting off its head, he will be able to put the king's crown on his head. Otherwise, despite being Laius's son, a born king, he will have killed his father in a duel and incestuously violated his mother, ending his days blind and exiled from his divine homeland.

I must clarify two points:

1. Does the manifestation of any extra-human being lead to the conquest of the astral serpent?
2. Isn't there a means for those who are alone, without advice or initiative, to open, however little, a way to the occult life?

I will answer these two questions:

The first answer is no, because the essence of what manifests itself is not always the same, but generally the genius of the pig is the swine, and the genius of the enlightened philosopher is a god.

The second answer is yes. There are many roads that lead to Rome. One must ardently desire; and when one least expects it, one of the doors to the divine realm opens unto those who desire courageously.

Ipse dixit. The spirit of occult initiation to the truth of the heavens manifests itself in proportion to mankind's self-improvement. When *one least expects it,* the genius of truth indicates a *master* behind a man who desires or a woman who prays. If the initiator is a real initiator and not a charlatan, the disciple perceives it, stretches out his hand to him, tries to fuse himself with the other's soul, and loves him. Love is divine; the disciple must love his master because without unlimited love, which tends toward good, the mind of the disciple will not understand the heart of the master.

I will stop here. I am neither a mystic nor an apostle. When one writes of heavenly things, the profane imagine one is dreaming. And yet, before inviting you to seek truth in cold blood, I will tell you:

Dream of loving a better world purely, sweetly, and poetically, and in your pious dream of an endless love you will become a poet; that is, a *poet* in the Orphic sense: you will have a feeling for sacred science, and you will sing the truth.

GENERAL PRINCIPLES

I divide *magic,* or arcane wisdom, into two major parts: *natural* magic and *divine* magic.

The former studies all phenomena caused by the occult qualities of the human organism and the way of obtaining them and reproducing them, within the limits of the organism employed as the means.

The latter is directed toward preparing the spiritual ascent of the seeker so as to enable the relationship between man and higher beings invisible to the common eye.

It is difficult to determine where the former ends and the latter begins because human nature is made in such a way that as it gradually achieves the freedom to operate through its latent virtues, it perfects itself and is able to perceive, to the same degree of its development, harmonies that cannot be perceived by common intelligence.

So, the two parts of *magic,* more often than not, walk hand in hand, and when we are able to perceive the guidance of a *genius* that may be outside of us, *our spirit* can work wonders.

The first part includes all physical phenomena that derive from the occult, from telepathy to faith healing to telekinesis.

Magic consists of a whole series of provable theorems and experiences with concrete effects; magical truths, however abstract, must have their evident proof in a *manifestation,* just as any truth of abstract mathematics has its mechanical applications.

We must, however, consider that progress in human research is strictly related to the passage of time, and if many *occult truths* can be proved by reasoning and hypotheses accepted by the experimental method, other truths can only be proved and considered absolute by observing their effects, because the abstract reasoning that would prove their existence is based on a *subtle* philosophy called *Hermetic,* which is understood only by the most advanced human intellects.

Scientific experiments and proofs can begin to study, for instance, telepathic phenomena, as many contemporaries who have not been initiated are doing in Europe and America; while other truths, such as *a corrupt man's shirt corrupts one who wears it* can only be demonstrated by the effects brought about by an operator or by the deep understanding of the law of contagion of virtues or vices that rules epidemics of vice and virtue.

I beg my readers not to be amazed if I use words that may seem strange, and to believe that I am not using them thoughtlessly, but weighing them carefully, and therefore their meaning must be interpreted attentively. When I said "epidemics of vice," I did not use a rhetorical device; but since our *magic* is synthetic, the fundamental synthetic principle of all laws is mathematically the same in all manifestations of the laws themselves; the law of fluidic contagion is constant in all different manifestations, and so just as we can have *epidemics* of diseases, we can likewise have *epidemics* of morality.

Perhaps I am the first who has a mind to present a whole body of doctrines, which are exact and immutable, and which belong to the protasis of secret and sacred science, which nobody has yet unveiled to the unprepared public, and which nobody can *unveil to anyone in its entirety.* Therefore, the disciple must not labor over the grammatical form of my phrases but must try to assimilate the hidden meaning that is essentially scientific.

Hermetic philosophy, which is the science engaged in investigations in the domain of the powers of the living human being that are not susceptible to verification, has its own way of looking at and experimenting with the existing forces and powers hidden and unknown to man.

Ours is a bold mission of propaganda for the principles of a future science of the human spirit, of the human essence in living man.

Our school, from the experimental point of view, is wholly materialistic, because the human being, body and mind, is only organized matter, or matter under organization. The normal phenomena we study in him are produced by his organism, and therefore by the matter of which he is made. Thought is possible, in all the different forms it adopts in us, in relation to the soundness of the organism (matter).

The true disciple of our school must pose himself problems and solve them by himself, because Hermeticism is not taught in the same way as any other discipline, from a textbook.

In the interior silence of the researcher there germinates the rich speculation of a most subtle philosophy, which creates and initiates the novice in magic and establishes a new vision of the universe, since it is necessary that the disciple of Hermeticism arrive by himself at the proof that ours is the only truth needed, and he can do so by moving from things below to things above, from Saturn to the Moon and from there to Mercury.

The master of Hermeticism expounds the elements of our theory and practice; the disciple works with them and studies them in his secluded laboratory and rises toward the truth of Hermetic practice and realization.

And in order for our school to have a gymnasium in which to pursue, through the first principles of the forces awakened in us, its own activity in the actual and practical realm of achievements, I have founded the Brotherhood of Myriam, the gathering of researchers of psychical science, whose activity affects the sick who come into contact with us and tries to cure them, or improve the state of their health, or soothe their pain and agony.

We are the first to take into consideration and examine a new principle of modern therapeutics: *the personal healing action of the physician, which modifies, enhances, and strengthens every medicine he prescribes, giving it a healing strength that prescriptions do not normally possess.*

Hermetic medicine—which is *spirit, intention, breath, image*—is distilled in the lunar body of the sick person, under a ray of powerful love, received between passion and faith; the cells of the tissues break up, reconstitute themselves, are healed, and life proceeds. The brain no longer feels pain; health, contentment, and peace of mind return; the miracle of *one thing* is accomplished as the miracle of love.

1. THE PERFECT MASTER

All creatures, before nature, are equal.

This means that the initial relationship between the creator and his creatures is constant. In fact, the law of evolution and the purpose of all human existence make all men equal in the sight of the *first cause;* whereas it is not the case that all men are equal in the physical domain, or in the domains of spirituality and morality.

In the absolute, that is, without the specification of time and space, the truth of the law is unquestionable; but where space and time are defined, as in nature, all men do not have the same rights.

Physically, men differ from each other in their size and beauty; spiritually, they differ in their more-or-less intellectual clear-sightedness.

In human society, governed by the base instincts (gluttony, lust, greed), *monarchies* are made up of a majority of those who are *physically* strongest. The weaker ones, willingly or unwillingly, are controlled by the stronger whose greater physical perfection, aided by the necessary intellectual capacity, gives them courage to rule and an intolerance of subjugation.

As in the visible world, so it is in the secret of the souls of the living, as far as the gifts and qualities of creatures are concerned. There are some natures that are spiritually advanced and others that are not; among the former, there are beaming searchlights and candles; and among the latter are poor, melancholy, and blind creatures who instinctively play with evil.

Religions, science, and governments are hierarchical because in the three worlds, the physical, the intellectual, and the spiritual, men differ from each other in the development of their tendencies or virtues.

The *Master* of occult teaching is the most advanced in comparison with neophytes.

No spiritual society can avoid this power of the *Master,* because he who sees and understands more clearly will always be the teacher of the spiritually young.

When a spiritual society is established, the *Master* becomes indispensable.

If the *Master* is a master in the widest sense of the word—that is, he clearly sees and understands the synthetic laws of the three worlds, physical, intellectual, and spiritual—his authority becomes absolute, and his teachings or rulings are *dogmatic.*

A *dogma* frightens without reason all the experimenters because they attach to this word a meaning it doesn't possess.

A *dogma is thought (cogitatio), clear-sightedness,* from the Greek *dokeo,* "to see."

The word in magic corresponds, as I said in the preparation section, to fluidic projection, whose laws we will study: a thought (*bene cogitatus*) that is synthetically coagulated in a master's psyche, concrete, harmonic, true, expressed in any graphic or aural form, is a *dogma,* because it is true in relation not only to philosophy, but also to morality and to practical realization; and it is immutable—that is, *infallible*—if it corresponds to a truth that is absolute, infallible, and immutable.

Darwin can dogmatize when he discovers and formulates a general law of nature, or Saint Paul when he defines charity, or Epictetus, the Stoic, when he defines the nature of things.

When religious or enlightened sects fall under the rule and dominion of leaders who do not have the virtue of seeing *the single light,* the source of all eternal wisdom, they become temporal and short-lived, and their pontiffs or grand masters dogmatize while remaining subjected to the relativity of time, and free reason rebels against them because the dogma lends itself to discussion and open examination.

A researcher in natural philosophy cannot be prevented from freely accepting or rejecting a statement of truth: the complete man, intellectually balanced, uses his reason before accepting or rejecting it; that is, he considers if the dogma has real value in terms of the eternal absolute. Nowadays when a philosopher concludes that *reason has killed dogma,* by dogma he means something that doesn't have an absolute value; on the contrary, since *dogma* is the evidence of truth, it can only be reasonable, and the contrary is true: *dogma is the reason for the truth.*

Magic has some fundamental truths or dogmas, which are the statements of synthetic laws on which all secondary truths depend.

The *Perfect Master* must have not only the power of vision, but also the power to pass on his spiritual gifts to others.

Many masters see and operate with clear and perfect understanding, but do not have the capacity for *giving, transferring,* and *conferring.*

In magic, any operator at all can temporarily *endow* men or things with certain virtues through processes that are part of elementary practice.

However, if any operator at all can give, not all operators can permanently *transfer or confer* the natural virtues they have acquired.*

Operators in magic must make use of the equilibrium resulting from their progress in order to neutralize all adverse forces, and in order to be considered *Perfect Masters* in the two parts of magic, they must possess negative and positive virtues, be able to to give and to take, to coagulate and dissipate all the psychic forces condensed around them to temporarily grant their own virtues to a student or deserving disciple when doing an investiture.

It is generally believed that science is learned out of books. But from the speculations of transcendental philosophy to the laws of mechanics, the only thing that teaches is realization or practice. Through reading one can reach a more or less clear idea of the *thing:* but only through operating under the direction of a Perfect Master can one develop the physical and psychical qualities that are of use in the reality of magic.

The *initiation* into the practice is the whole of all the operations

---

*The reader is advised to note that I am speaking of natural virtues and not of theurgic properties, which belong to the highest stage of magical development.

that a Perfect Master carries out on a disciple to grant, confer, confirm, and develop the virtues hidden in his common human organism.

Now we come to the problem of the school, and to the mystery that in all times has formed the secret of magical sects and religions. Let us concentrate all our attentions on this.

$$\mathbb{D}$$

2. THE DISCIPLE

In the present literary climate, in which every ordinary person, in the light of equality and liberty, wants to express his personal opinion about the occult sciences, the word *initiate* has acquired a very elastic meaning.

Let's come to an agreement of terms before we go on. Where a master exists, there also exist *disciples*.

An invisible thread binds the disciples to the master and to each other, *even without their knowledge*.

Imagine a circle: place the master in the center, or $\odot$, and all around the circumference place the disciples, or $\mathbb{D}$. Hence the concept of the Mystic Rose, many petals around a bud, which is its soul, spirit, force, and intelligence.

Therefore, by *initiate* we must understand the disciple who has emerged from the dead water of the masses and has come within the zone of radiation from the center; this can be better explained by saying that whoever has the ability, has done all the work of purification and preparation upon a neophyte in order to detach him completely from the common milieu, drawing him out of the stream of the vulgar masses and elevating him to purer waters, to which the mob cannot rise owing to their natural weight—owing to that inflexible and inexorable law that condemns lead to sink and leaves to float.

Proposition 1—Fluidic changes shine forth in the
outer habits of the disciple.
Generally, the contrast between the new and the old life, between the transformed man and the common man, is enormous.

The fluidic changes of the disciple have such a great effect upon his exterior, they shine forth in his outer habits in such a way that common men, that is, those who do not understand *secret things,* generally consider extravagant those men and women who devote themselves to magic.

This is not only a logical but a necessary state of affairs; because if a man is made in the same way as the huge mass of creatures who populate the visible world, he cannot approach the invisible world and its creatures. The conflict between the visible and invisible worlds has as its basis the passion of temporality: that is, the visible world feeds on the constant fear of not having and not possessing; while the invisible world lives in the eternal certainty of taking when one wants and when one needs it.

I will illustrate with two examples.

The vulgar man loves a woman not only because men love women but also because of a sense, which cannot be confessed, and which exists in every animal and in every human group, of rating himself the most virile of men. It is the most natural thing in the world both for matter to claim its moment of dominion over intellect and for the reasonable man to give in to this momentary triumph of the flesh, once a partner has been chosen not only for her bodily perfection but also for her homogeneous and attractive moral kindness. But a common man doesn't stop here, at what should be his point of arrival. He becomes a Casanova toward *all* women who can stimulate his self-esteem; he must sniff the scent of every flower he sees, out of male vainglory, always behaving like a rapacious Attila toward all honest women who do not pay homage to him. Youth, adults, and old men feel it is their duty to degrade the essentially aristocratic human nature (which is divine in origin) of man in a muddy morass of base animal instincts that brand him forever a stinking goat.

As soon as a man peeps into the realm of mysteries and shadows, the divine principle, which is within him, that is his spirit, acquires supremacy over his humanity, and those who do not recognize his aristocracy think of him in the same way as the roosters think of the little capons in the henhouse.

Common men love money. Key to all the holy arks for the vulgar, gold is a king before whom all the feelings of feigned honesty, all the false moral forces bow down. I need not give an example: everybody knows that for the masses money represents the most powerful talisman, bringing the serenity of a comfortable life, domestic peace, the satisfaction of all whims, the sweetness of all hired lovers.

But the disciple of divine wisdom, aspiring only to a higher ideal, dethrones this king and continues on his way, with his cloak, stick, and knapsack, like a stoic who despises this idol, before whom, as before a beautiful woman, everybody bows down.

An ordinary woman wants only to satisfy her vanity. Elegant in her ways, in her dress and hairstyles, she continually dreams of enslaving all men and of making all her friends and acquaintances green with envy. But the woman who, as a petal of the Mystic Rose, comes under the influence of a master, little by little, imperceptibly but progressively, gives up her vanity, and the eye of her mind soars ever higher.

Proposition 2—The disciple's fatal test is in his separation from the master.

The two streams—the false vulgar one, deceptive and very powerful, and the true and incorruptible occult one—work upon the disciple in the same way as two magnets of equal and opposing force work upon a piece of iron placed at an equal distance from their extremes. The piece of iron has no will, and when it is placed at an equal distance between the two forces it doesn't move. But the disciple has a will, which the master must never override, and this will pushes him a little toward one, a little toward the other, and so the disciple's soul, until his triumph or fall, knows a horrible torment, torn between believing in the promise of the light and feeling the attraction of the demon of the common stream.

As long as the disciple is within the influence of the radiation of the master, he absorbs the latter's occult virtues, and the vulgar stream has no hold on him because his master's influence destroys it completely.

But as soon as the disciple is left to stand alone, he is subject to reactions, and two principles are at war within him: the divine occult one and the worldly one. The latter is fed by the vulgar stream, it becomes overpowering, and while the master draws back, if the disciple doesn't continue to work for his own salvation, he is submerged by the tide of vulgarity and either goes mad or kills himself.

To sum up:

(a) the disciple can consider himself an *initiate* as soon as he withdraws from the common stream;
(b) those who are initiates in occult sciences and practices necessarily end by clashing with the public's profane opinions;
(c) the disciple's supreme test is in his separation from the master, and if he doesn't possess the strength to carry out his creation independently, he falls into the common stream and is destroyed.

Proposition 3—Fluidic equilibrium equates with physical equilibrium.

Those who want to study magic and its practice must be sound in body and mind. On presenting himself at the threshold of the temple, the disciple must bring with him all his flourishing and balanced forces and spontaneously renounce all the illusions he has cultivated up to that time.

Soundness of body is indispensable—that is why all rules of magic teach that when one is not in perfect health, one doesn't *work*—because each practice bears the indelible stamp of the practitioner's state of equilibrium or lack of equilibrium. Now, as the deformity of the body gives rise to an almost permanent state of fluidic deviation, so temporary infirmities determine a passing stage of lack of equilibrium in the practitioner. It is not only physical defects that impede the study and magical practices but also the state of incontinence, both in men and in women.

In operant and natural magic, *absolute chastity* is not necessary, provided the disciple can be *continent* during the periods of his working. In divine magic, chastity is a necessary condition without which all high intelligences fly away; that is why marriage between an initiate and an ordinary woman impedes the development of divine magic.

Proposition 4—Lifestyle has a capital influence on the nutrition and development of the fluidic being.

Along with the sexual act, all other outward acts, in common with other animals, have a great influence on the disposition, growth, and power of the disciple's fluidic body.

It is absolutely not necessary to delude yourself about the omnipotence of the value of the soul, if the soul (intelligence and conscience) is not really trained to dominate the physical body, which it can modify as much as the character.

The program of preparation for magical power and pure Hermeticism can be explained quite briefly: *make the integrative powers of human intellect (will) the absolute master of the animal frame, making it a prompt and obedient slave to the psychodynamic authority that is within us; rid yourself of all obstacles to the free exercise of intelligent will over the body, the necessary instrument for human life; liberate yourself from worldly needs.*

The choice of food must be scientifically made by the master according to the disciple's animal economy, after a careful study of all his tendencies and the well-defined characteristics of his fluidic inclinations.

I must warn you once and for all that I am publishing the absolute principles of this unknown science, and that a full application of *all* its precepts is only for those who have got well ahead in natural and divine magic and who do not suffer at all in doing all these things, indeed would suffer if they did the opposite. But that the disciples, on the contrary, especially the young, can start by degrees toward the realization of these precepts under the guidance of a master and by themselves, so that the abrupt transition from an ordinary lifestyle to the well-structured diet does not produce changes that are temporarily painful to the animal organism.

Sleep must not last very long, because the state of sleep in the human organism greatly contributes to making the animal organism heavy; it makes all the bodily components heavy, and the fluidic potential numb.

To this end, I suggest a hard camp bed and a light blanket in a very spacious room, where no lamp or candle must burn while the disciple is asleep. A man who is mystically asleep must reenter the total blackness of the astral and while the organism recovers its strength he, that is, the intelligent man, must attempt to pass through the black zone into the white astral light. This happens instinctively in those whose psychic development is advanced, even if they belong to the mob; so much so that prophetic dreams or dreams of white light are just successful attempts by the sleeper's psyche to enter the world of astral light, uncontaminated by earthly pollution.

The animal strength of sleep must be recovered properly because man's fluidic organism, which takes vitality from his physical envelope, must not find it tired or overfed or numb. If you examine the rules of all the monastic religious orders, whose founders were recognized revealers of old forms of magic or wisdom, you will realize that the logical, exclusively scientific rules of magical practice not only coincide with the monastic ones but also with the precept of strict hygiene, which approximates what is currently taught in European schools.

The ventilation of the bedroom, the hard bed, the blanket, which must be neither too heavy nor too light, the cleanliness of the bed linen, the extreme cleanliness of the body, which is achieved by baths in the morning and evening, are simply in accordance with the strictest rules of hygiene, which, written down in books, are not easily put into practice.

I will now advise the practitioner even about the color of the walls and ceiling of the room in which he sleeps: colors, through the sense of sight, have a direct effect upon the brain, the cerebellum and the nerves, as we shall study later; colored paints produced from mineral or vegetable matter, which to different extents may influence the brain by inhalation of their vapors, even through the skin, have the worst effect.

Those who have the means and opportunity should replaster their bedroom walls and ceiling and whitewash them, avoiding lead-based white paint. The color white is the best suited to psychic sensations of visual origin and mystically it is projected as the image of purity; indeed it is to be noted that, if the color white in magical and religious symbolism is related to purity and virginity, this is due to the development of the magical truth that color *confers its virtue according to the idea and quality attributed to it.**

Furniture, garments even when washed, cloth, blankets, and chairs keep the mark or, better, the smell of he who used them, and are generators of fluidic contagion under the same general law that experimenters have attributed to contagion by microorganisms. He who can, therefore, prepares a room for himself, exclusively for his own fluidic life; for the practice of magic, he should *replace everything,* from the largest to the most insignificant item of human life, and should refuse as impure any intrusion of another person's fluid, except for masters much advanced in the art *when they don't operate in an impure way,* since, if people better than you come to your place, you have much to gain and nothing to lose.

In this context, I must hint at the substances used to purify places in old books of instructions, now superseded, such as incense, aloe, sulfur, benzoin, pitch, sandalwood, fragrant herbs, flowers—which present-day experimental science wants to replace scientifically with carbolic acid and other similar disinfectants.

The substances, which have been used since ancient times as disinfectants, were used by priests in bygone ages. The Magi of ancient Persia, even those who traditionally knelt beside Christ's crib, used incense, myrrh, sandalwood, and precious resins, as did the magicians of the Middle Ages, and as modern practitioners do both in the East and the West, because the scientific concept from which both ancient

---

*White is the symbol of natural purity because any color whatsoever is its contrary, and the fusion of all contraries is achieved in its absolute contrary, black.

and modern magicians proceed is one and the same. The fundamental action on which rests the science of what exists is this: *thought, fluidically, is generative; each realized projection has its origin not only in the thought of the creator but also in the projecting instrument.*

I will illustrate with an example.

An operator's will, conscious or unconscious, is the cause of every imponderable fluidic disturbance in an environment. As long as thought is aided by a projecting instrument of the human organism, the reality, sooner or later, becomes a fact. The disturbance generates a physical disturbance, which at the extreme suppresses animal life, which means *death*.

Now let's see how to neutralize the prime cause from the opposite point of view. Act on the practitioner's will, either by influencing his projecting device *or by isolating your own fluidic radiation so that the harmful and deadly projections don't reach their target.*

Perfumes, from the subtlest to the strongest, through a direct action on our organism and on the organism of those who enter a specific place, are capable of developing such a preponderance of fluid in us that others' *attempts at fluidic contagion are in vain.*

From this point of view, we mustn't make fun of the ancients who purified houses with incense—nor should we consider its use illogical in religious rites.

Now going back to what I was saying about the purification of the place where the disciple must establish the source of his purity, fumigations methodically carried out are advisable; the best judge of them can only be the master or a brother who is more advanced in the study and practice of magic, *since perfumes and fumigations have different effects depending on who uses them, the time when they are used, the place, and the practitioner.*

Clearly, it is understood if the aspiring magician wanted to practice purification in all stages of his life, he should confine himself to a monastic existence.

But social life demands that man doesn't retire completely from the world for very many reasons; first of all because, as I said before, the saint has nothing to do with the magician. Whereas asceticism demands and fosters solitude, magical life cannot demand perfect, complete, and perpetual solitude, owing to the very nature of magical art and practice. The ascetic aims for individual improvement; he is passive, he doesn't look for others on whom to exercise his intellect and force. The magician, however, who is active par excellence, can neither act nor develop his force except through other men and living things.

In order for you not to think that this life of isolation, which I am advising must mean shutting yourself off completely from the world, I want to further add: anyone who reaches perfection has, as his mission, to use his conquest, if not for the good of nations and mankind, at least for the good of his neighbor whom he must help in all the circumstances of life.

This concept of human solidarity is based on this sense of brotherhood; thus, any aspirant to magical power who hopes to succeed in his ideal turns into a little messiah, a bringer of peace and comfort.

The would-be magician, in order to live in the *world of causes,* must be isolated, and, in order to manifest and develop his powers, must maintain social relations.

When he *lives* in the extra-human world, all that is matter and human fluid offends him: even the light of the sun, which greets the happy days of spring, even the kiss of a woman who loves him; but in order to *use* his powers he needs human society.

The regimen of his human life must always represent the most complete activity. To live for the body *and* for the spirit is problematic; it means action in perpetual motion until the palingenesis of matter and the triumph of the spirit over all is reached; until his conscious liberation from the ties of the earth; and until he completes his evolution toward the divine central principle, which the masses call God, but which in magic is called *Tetragrammaton,* which means "a word of four letters," because this central power has no name, and in Hebrew it is designated this way.

Morning ablutions, baths, isolation at certain hours and on certain days, purify even the purified man who is momentarily fouled by the overpowering effluvium of human society into which he goes to exercise his power and his mission. The scents that come from the fire purify the air he breathes of any fluidic coagulation since the vapors of the scents have in them not only the virtue of the resins, the barks, the wood, and the fragrant herbs, but they also confirm to our senses how the fire, by burning wood, resins, barks, and herbs, transmits to the dead waters of coagulated forces its purifying and renovating movement, and is the origin of every change that prevents the rot of astral stasis.

Proposition 5—The supply of fluid is proportional to the nutrition of the animal organism.

But if sexual continence and the purification of the environment in which the aspiring magician takes refuge have a great importance in his fluidic life, and if the perpetual activity of his body and spirit prepares him for his progress in the field of uncommon and extra-human phenomena, nothing is more necessary to the development of fluidic life than ordinary nutrition.

It is ordinarily believed that the human body has only one way of feeding: through the esophagus. And it is believed that the food eaten is transformed into blood and consequently into nervous or intellectual energy. This is not the complete process of nutrition of the two material bodies (physical and fluidic) that interpenetrate each other in the human organism. The nutrition that is fit for the former, is almost always to be avoided for the latter, and what we call the *disease of the century, or neurasthenia,* the source of myriad nervous disturbances, originates not only in the society in which we live but also, and mainly, in the wrong nutrition of our organism, to which are given or attributed artificial needs that are not naturally there.

The physical nutrition of the human body depends *not only on the quality and quantity of food* eaten but on the vapors the body absorbs during daily life. The absorbing power is particular to the fluidic body and its vampiric [*vampirica*] kind of nutrition, and, whereas the material body digests and transforms masticated food into chyle, the fluidic body takes its life from aspiration and through the nourishment of the nervous system and the soft ganglionic parts of the physical body.

I have said that the body takes nourishment in several ways and that the digestive tract is not the only way of getting nutrition. I will now indicate that, more than the esophagus, stomach, or intestines, the first and most important apparatus of nourishment in the developed man is the psychic apparatus or vampiric psychic irradiation. Observe the normal animal nutrition of the range of so-called reasoning bipeds: starting from the idiot go through the whole range up to the philosopher and the ascetic, and you will find that where low animal instincts of vulpine voracity predominate (the *idiot*), everything that is psyche or intelligence in the advanced beast, is atrophied, or better yet, still not developed; and in the opposite case the contrary is true: that in those most highly developed and advanced (*philosophers, thinkers*) everything that can be related to base animality is in continual regression.*

Step by step, as intellectuality evolves in man, his greed for food decreases. And when the intelligent principle takes the upper hand, its bonds with the animal body are loosened and, while the latter wastes away, the former becomes stronger.

But this must not be the goal of those who aspire to magical practices; for just as solitude and company must be the two poles of the existence of an active magician, so his physical body must represent the most robust container for his spirituality; and to this state of perfect

---

*Gymnastics in European schools is the theoretical antidote to the quantity of poison that boys absorb from their books: in other words, physical exercise should balance intellectual exercise so that a boy's physical and mental development should proceed hand in hand; but, in practice, even in schools, we can see that this doesn't happen. Those in whom an athletic body combines with a bright intelligence are few and far between, and commonly when one is predominant the other is deficient. For the perfect education of a boy who has a normal mental development, instead of exercises done at home or in the gymnasium, I suggest sports in which mental interest is always kept alive: soccer, for instance, or riding or fencing, swimming, and long walks.

equilibrium between the two extremes, which fight for supremacy, the magician owes his perfect bodily health, and to the most complete state of realization of this equilibrium he owes the health of his psychic faculties. His nutrition must be in line with his work and his consumption: there is nothing more scientific than the intuitive work in the choice of food in a disciple who has just begun to practice.

The advice I give to those who start is to be frugal. Wish for simple, natural food, prepared without too much fuss. Prefer vegetables, avoid as much as possible game and blood. Enjoy the odor of a cask full of purple wine, but drink it very moderately and refuse liquor and alcoholic drinks.

Eat whatever you like, but be frugal. Drink whatever you need, but in moderation. Sleep when you can, but be industrious.

Be abstemious or indulgent at will, so as to become master of your deeds.

If you suffer, you will say that the cause is in yourself, and you will look for it until you find it.

Correct your ways, choose the right path, and wipe out all the stains of badness in you.

Fasting is a symbolic rebirth of the body, a rebirth to the life of light; it is a moral and material regeneration. It is a most powerful aid to the development and liberty of the astral body.

3. INTELLIGENT POWERS, FORCES, AND CREATIONS

We have studied the Perfect Master (No. 1 ☉)—we have put forward the principal conditions of the disciple, which will be helpful to his development (No. 2 ☽): now we are ready to study in an elementary way the problem of the extra-human, the superhuman, and the occult human.

The reader must remember what I alluded to but did not enlarge upon about the invisible world in the *preparation* section to the present discussion; but he must proceed step-by-step.

The spiritual education of the disciple has two aims:

1. To improve the psychophysical conditions of the aspiring magician so that he may come nearer to an ideal organic perfection.
2. To make him sensitive to the influence of any outside physical or intelligent irradiations.

According to the constitution that nature equipped the disciple with, the results will be maximal or minimal, but they cannot nor will they ever arrive at nothing; because as the state of purification progresses in a man, he anticipates his life in the *spirit;* but instead of being completely born in the invisible world, he participates in human and ultrahuman life at the same time.

This is a first essential point on which the disciple must focus his attention.

The law of progressive evolution governs all the things that have been created and that *can be created*. If the death of a man represents his birth to a second life, as the death of uterine life announces his birth to life on earth, it clearly means what the human spirit is when it is still in a man's material body, in comparison to a fetus in a woman's womb.

The fertilized egg in the incubation period of the mother hen represents, analogously, what the human spirit still in a man's material body is. The basic difference lies in this: the fetus in the womb and the chicken in the egg cannot, just as the human spirit cannot, communicate with the physical world outside the womb and the shell, which means, in the levels of low animality, that spirituality, which breaks down all physical obstacles, is embryonic.

Magical education aims to free the spirit imprisoned in a man's body by very strong bonds so that he may, freely, anticipate his third existence, or second intelligent life.*

---

*The first existence is that of the embryo.

Magic, in so far as its teaching, practice, and realization, has always maintained as much, and many religious myths have perpetuated it through the darkness of remote ages, that the human body represents the vessel or container of the divine, intelligent principle that is incarnated, that has entered earthly matter, to sublimate certain forces in the direction of divine realization. But since this teaching does not belong to the elements but to high magical theurgy, I will only call the researcher's attention to the arrangement, structure, and nutrition of the human *psyche.*

Break open a fertilized egg and you will find (1) the fertilizing coagulate, (2) the yolk, and (3) the albumen. When the chick is hatched—by an alchemical miracle of maternal or artificial warmth—the three elements contained in the shell have been transformed into an animal (which no one could have imagined), an animal, strangely enough, that, twenty-one days before the miracle, no one would have thought the seed fertilizing the yolk and albumen of the egg would have the power to give life. Now, the birth of man to his second life must absorb all earthly materiality, in the same way as the chick took nourishment from the contents of the egg; the human spirit becomes *disembodied*—that is, it is *created spirit*—when it has absorbed the materials that nourished it. In every man, in fact, the natural process is this: the physical body is consumed (old age) and one is born into the life of the spirit (death). Natural magic aims at a great realization, which is astounding, unbelievable, in our times: I am talking about *creating the state of spirit in man while his body is not absorbed* (like the chick absorbs the contents of the egg). The body serves, on the contrary, as a container of material supplies, continually renewed and never completely absorbed,* until and as long as he needs them.

How all this is done is easy to understand: either you have contact with a man who has reached such an advanced level of development and who can communicate the same properties to you or confirm them in you; or you possess, by grace of·God, the clear vision to intuit the laws

---

*The elixir of life has this ideal foundation: constant renewal of the matter of the human body to avoid its stasis and its collapse.

of this secret alchemy of the human spirit; *or you work for many years, many long years, and then achieve it, through hard work and perseverance, when you least expect it.*

The last two methods are the commonest, because meeting a perfect master on your way, who actually gives you this starting point of development, indicates itself a stroke of grace, which in the human world has no correlative, because this gift cannot be paid for in this world's money. That man gives you immortality and becomes your true father in spiritual eternity and you must learn by contact and from the master to live your own life and fully grow.

As a matter of fact, we sometimes meet creatures, male or female, who are exceptional in the development of their spiritual state; in this way the states of *natural mediumship* appear, and the visible evidence of this in certain beings is their natural inclination toward religious or amorous asceticism.

Where the development of the psycho-fluidic organism does not develop in harmony with the physical body, the animal life of the individual is very abnormal, and the nervous disorders and the many pathological phenomena show to the world of the ignorant that one is dealing with a crackpot. That is why certain cases of madness were sacred in ancient religions; that is why the enlightened religions prescribed that those who had a tendency toward sacred matters should be immediately admitted to the priestly order, so that the premature development of their fluidic self would not have to struggle against a profane life. That is why many men who have applied themselves body and soul to flush out the devil, without rules or a guide or an extra-human divine intellectual aid, have been struck by physical accidents or diseases that have made them into subjects for observation in the anatomy room.

There is nothing simpler than the practice of Allan Kardec's spiritualism,* and yet I invite researchers to observe closely, in those who

---

*[A. Kardec, *Il Libro degli Spiriti, Il Libro dei Medium* (The Book of Spirits, the Book of Mediums) (Rome: Edizioni Mediterranee, 1972). —*Ed.*]

become the most highly developed mediums, all the alterations in the medium's body as he progresses and, at the same time, continues his worldly life. Some start to go pale, others show heart or breathing trouble, others have stomach or nerve trouble; none of the advanced mediums can say: "I am physically the vigorous man I once was."

But is it true that those who follow the practices of spiritualism to develop their latent mediumistic powers run the risk of killing themselves, or of at least nervous disorders? Is it true, in short, that those who devote themselves to the practices of divine sciences become physically and intellectually ill? This is incontestably true, *if the development of a man's spirit is not in accord with a new regimen for his human life.*

Therefore, magic, through the gradually adjusted regimen for living it prescribes for disciples, foretells a state of equilibrium between the spirit and its physical vessel; from that state—the perfect health of the body, while the spirit is purified and floats in higher regions—the forces of the fluidic body take exceptional vigor. Illness in the physical body of a magician always represents a mistake he has made in the domain of the fluidic body, so close is the relationship in him between fluidic development and physical health.

Now we face the problem: once the disciple's body has been prepared sufficiently to render it sensitive to any sensation not perceived by other men, what does he see in the invisible world?

First of all, does another world really exist, or is it rather an invention of the sick mind?

Natural magic teaches, and everyday experience proves, that beyond the forces studied by physics and applied by mechanics there exist *forces* that physics and mechanics are unaware of, and these forces by conventional names have been called *hyperphysical,* that is, above the physical. It seems useless to prove the scientific error of a name that cannot stand up to our examination.

Physis, from the Greek, means "nature." All forces are included in nature independent from the intellectual principle that animates them: sound, warmth, electricity, light. The science of physics studies these forces very imperfectly because it limits its studies to the laws in their experimental effects, while coming back to the *unity of motion*. It should study the laws of their creation—modifications or ways of being of the forces in nature—that our animal organism liberates.

If by the indefinite search for the source, which is the mother of all the manifestations of all physical forces and energies, you mean to reach unity, I do not think you can imagine a more synthetic thing than magnetism in nature, which is always considered magically as energy, force, warmth, sound, electricity, time, space, dimension, motion, life: the expression of all that appears in so many different manifestations of the intelligent physical nature of the perceptible world.

From what is occult in us emanates the variety of forces summed up in the word *life,* from animal sensation to thought, to the idea, to the image conceived, to the organic preserving magnetism that transforms and creates.

Consequently, magnetism is the synthesis of the energy and life that makes a human unity. Magnetism is indefinable, life is indefinable; the former, coming from a universal source, is the father and supreme center of all forces in perceptible nature; the latter, created by the former, evolves or stops for incomprehensible reasons. Therefore, we all possess a magnetic power—but in different proportions according to our natural constitution—that can manifest itself without the individual being aware of it.

The animal machine emits a perceptible amount of sound, warmth, magnetism, and electricity, and an imperceptible amount of light.

Now, if these exclusively physical forces are reduced in the human organism to the movement of blood and the intelligent principle that moves the whole, we find the mystery of *vitality* and of *life-motion,* which is synchronous with *motion,* which represents, in the abstract, the unity of mechanical forces in visible nature.

Animal life (or better, *vital animal impulse*) starts, transmitted by the father in an ecstasy that lasts but a moment, in a fertilized ovum, and ends when the last tear runs down the dead man's cheeks; but nothing can stop us believing that the motion transmitted through the act of generation does not go on even after the death of the material body visible to all, in a third fluidic body that is its successor. This motion (*movement-unity*), together with all its manifestations (differently named as psychic, magnetic, hypnotic, or nervous forces, and so forth) are not above nature but inside *physical nature,* and therefore they are not hyperphysical but physical—we can simply call them *occult* because their action is not perceived by all organized beings.

In order to be scientifically rigorous, not even the word *occult* should be used because all the forces not yet studied by experimental science are not occult in their effects but only in their laws of production, as electricity was *occult* until Volta invented the electric battery.

Now, since all the forces in nature are measured, studied, and identified on the basis of their perceptible effects, it would be self-evident, given only the *effects* of electricity, heat, and light, to deny that there is a world of brute forces that human intelligence can enslave and bend to its will. Through the observation of all these phenomena of heat, light, magnetism, and sound that occur in the small world (*microcosm*) of the individual man, we see in abbreviated form the world of vital human forces.

However, the meaning of the question "Does another world exist?" doesn't refer to physical forces, because physics doesn't attract dreamers, but to the existence of a *world of individuals who have already lived on the earth* or of beings who have never lived in human form and yet possess reason and will.

Materialists answer no; spiritualists answer yes. The former state that *anything that does not fall under the five senses of the human animal is untrue.* The latter, on the contrary, maintain that the five senses known in man represent what man has in common with inferior animals and that one must take into account the *human spirit or intelligence,* which represents a sixth sense, intuitive and clairvoyant, which is the property of evolved man and which must be taken as the rule and basis of any appraisal of *existing things that do not fall under the five senses.*

Let's for a while leave materialists and spiritualists alone, and let's ask ourselves what is truth. The five human senses, the powerful weapon of the sensists, often deceive us: one random test with a sensitive, impressionable subject, even before he is put into a hypnotic sleep, is enough to convince us that the animal senses are the most imperfect of all created things. The state of hypnosis, even superficial, can easily be used to alter the normal functions of the senses in a sensitive subject. It is clear that not all hypnotized subjects can easily see with their fingertips, but all of them taste in a glass of clear water what we want an experimental subject to taste in it: fresh water acquires the taste and properties of castor oil; a basket of flowers can assume for the subject all possible forms. Now, experimental science has not yet understood in what place and in what proportion the most unexpected phenomena of hypnosis or credulity can be found in a society of reasoning men, so as to determine the true level of normal *natural sensation* that is free from any outside influence.

Physiology assigns all central functions of the senses to the brain, but whether the brain or the cerebellum or the medulla oblongata or the sympathetic nervous system is the center of all external impressions, it is certain that the animal senses are a poor and paltry thing that easily deceive, and betray the truth in any examination of existence. External sensations arrive or do not arrive at the sensitive center according to whether the delicate nerves carry the impression from the periphery to the center or not.

If we think, it is because we hear, touch, see, taste, and smell— or we have the relative ideas, the mind (*mens*), that is, intelligence in its human mechanism, which cannot neglect perception. There is no thought that, directly or indirectly, does not refer to sensory memories. Don't believe, O man, that you are soul and body; consider yourself a unity, like the universe.

I said: let us leave materialists and spiritualists alone; if we reason without the passion of an argument to support and defend, just for the sake of discussion, or because it is our profession, or because we follow a school, and if we isolate ourselves from the humbug that men of letters, experimenters, and philosophers utter around us, we may wonder if each nervous impression that affects the centers of our sensations, results from a truth, a will, or an illusion.

Where do you think you will find the truth? Above all sensations? In this case the physical senses are not a reference point for the impression of *that which seems to be.* In the exclusive domain of the senses free from any outside influences? In this case it is the mind, the reason, the spirit that speaks. Below all physical impressions? But who guarantees that we do not cut off the truth, creating for ourselves a sensation in our sensory center that does not come at all from the periphery? And is it true that the path of sensations begins at the periphery and arrives at the sensory centers? And who can assure us that it is not the other way round and that from the sensory centers they arrive at the periphery? Or when is the first thing true, and when the second?

The happiest men are those who either do not think or have no time to think; the one who would like to discuss philosophically the questionable aspects of that which appears to us, and whether it *might* or *might not be*—that one would end up in the madhouse. Now, occult philosophy (I mean the elementary kind and not the most complex, about which one does not write) goes back to the origin of the action of the senses on the intellectual creative power and reduces fundamental truth to a formula: *each sensation is an idea and each idea is a sensation; the idea of a being is a being, and the central power of all that was and can be created in the universe* (macrocosm) *or in man* (microcosm) *is the being,* at the same time creator and creation, that is, maker and made, tree and fruit.*

Is such a fundamental axiom difficult, dear reader? I do not ask you to discuss it, but to meditate upon it serenely, in all the calm hours of your spirit when the divine light smiles on your intelligence, and when you need consolation for the fact that from time immemorial all the strife of human thought in relation to *elusive reality* has been the same,

---

*[*Ente* (Italian), comes from Latin *ens,* "being." —*Trans.*]

in all epochs and for all civilizations, until the secret philosophy of the magicians has set forth the first esoteric truth in the form of the mystical triangle common to all classical religions and to all philosophical and initiatic sects.

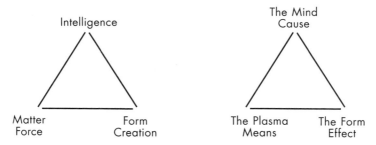

To reduce these three philosophical factors to the esoteric language of the dogmatic churches is the easiest thing.

The father, intelligence, mind, the informing spirit, the sensory center are synonyms for the upper vertex of this triangle; the other two vertices represent the Son (or forming matter, or periphery) and the Holy Spirit (the vehicle of human creative force from the active center, the Father).

Take note, dear readers, that I am reducing the occult religious symbolism to an explanation of the form of *Absolute Truth* in all its possible aspects.

Now turn the triangle upside down:

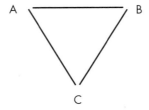

and placing in vertex *C* the central power receiving sensations from the periphery, you will find in the inverted triangle all that corresponds to form, thought, and the religious concept of the devil of the Catholic Church in this symbol of absolute blindness in which the sensory centers are under the blind influence of the peripheral extremes *A* and *B:* it is matter creating its *God without light.*

Let us examine words. The number 3, to which the planetary sign of Mercury ☿ corresponds, includes all the three terms of the triangle in its upright position: *intelligence, forces, and creations;* or the cause, the means, and the effect, that is the whole work of a realization both in natural and divine magic.

To create, the theologians explain, means *drawing something out of nothing.* But this is not true, because the concept of the *universe* or *cosmos* is the abstract of all that has been and will be, including the *prime intelligence* that animates everything. *Creation,* according to the sacred symbolism, is the action of the supreme potentiality of divine Intelligence upon unsublimated matter, which produces a *form,* which is nothing but an indication of the reforming will. Even if we want to take sacred traditional books literally, God *created* Man, mixing the slime of the earth with his breath: both the slime and the breath existed before man, and they were put together and mixed by the will to *create* a more perfect form of animal that would be closer to the thought that gave it form. And this *man created* by a supreme will has passed down to us the impulse of the divine will that created him . . . and we were created by our fathers exactly in the same way as the first and oldest of our ancestors was created by God's will, exactly in the same way as we create a child by mixing the slime of the earth (the act of animal copulation) with a certain *spirit of life,* which the sensists will never catch, because this *spirit of life* is liberated in that physiological moment in which materialist philosophy in absorbed by the senses, in the spasm of love and of the libido, and spiritualist doctrine is kidnapped in the spiritual ecstasy, which produces quite material effects after nine months, if not before.

Therefore, to *create* is not to draw something out of nothing, it is to give life and form, thought and will, spirit and essence and appearance.

If mankind did not think only of getting rich and of the refined enjoyment of the most delicate and highly developed sensations, it would not be going far from the source of absolute truth because occult philosophy, which is the true, the only, the immutable reason behind all things, determines the two currents thus, in common terms:

(a) The pleasure in the life of the senses is the result of all the actions of the outside world on the inert intellectual center.

(b) The creative act, the true imitation of God, the prime Intelligence, is, contrary to any profane pleasure, the preponderance of the intellectual center (*intelligent will*) over the extremes at the periphery in contact with the outside world.

Hence the difference between the initiate into natural magic and the ordinary man. The former has his thinking center (*intelligence, force, will, and action*) perfectly in accordance with conditions in (b), is free from the world around him and capable of producing the phenomenon of the realization of his will; while the latter is totally under the influence of any intellectual stimulus that comes to him through external sensation.

I recommend the reader who really wishes to progress to study closely this fundamental part of the mechanics of impressions and will whose philosophical foundation I have explained in the same way as is taught in the Kabbalah,* the book of the philosophy of the absolute and the relative. But I leave the way open for those who wish to study the Kabbalah in its parts, and I draw out and spread its precepts in this survey of the elements of the secret science of the magicians so that the application of the precepts will be clear, and so that I will not continually hear people say that the occult sciences are a veritable fraud done by those people who profit from the credulity of others. Better, I intend to throw in the furrow of studious people, prepared by the skepticism of our schools not to believe, the prolific seed of an integral or scientific theocracy that will create, for the peoples of the future, a state of merciful well-being throughout its civil organization.

---

*[Gershom Scholem. *Kabbalah* (New York: Meridian, 1978). —*Ed.*]

But let us not get away from our intuitive progression.

So, it is not the senses that lie, but the sensations elaborated in the conscious centers of a man who is not free to judge.

The physical senses are for men the only reference point of reality; but the sensory impressions acquire their value according to the state of consciousness and the psychical neutrality of the sensitive subject. In order to understand the real nature of things, we need a state of perfect neutrality, which is produced by a perfect equilibrium within ourselves.

Once we have established the principle that human senses deceive the passive sensory centers, the problem "Does another world of reasoning, invisible, and willing creatures exist?" cannot be demonstrated or appreciated and discussed using animal senses, and we have to go against the current of low sensations indirectly from the center to the periphery in order to be conscious of sensations that are different from the ordinary.

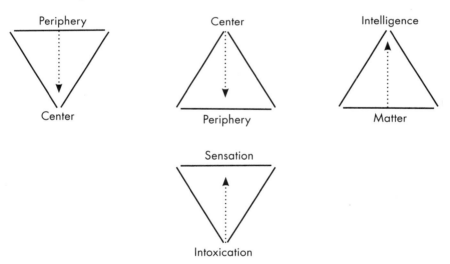

Magnetize a sensitive subject. Charging him with your fluid, or hypnotizing him by mechanical means, you will isolate him from outside sensations. This means that you will produce the temporary phenomenon of freeing his intelligent sensory center from outside influences. Free from outside sensations, the psychical center of the subject is to the psychical center of an ordinary man as the mind of the man with an empty stomach is to the mind of the same man who has copiously abused intoxicating drinks. The phenomenon of lucidity, of clairvoyance, is obtained. *The impression of a fluidic thought or the evoked image of an existing thing* immediately reflects on the intelligent sensory center of the subject who communicates, not with the senses of his physical body, but with the mind (thought-force) of the one who magnetized him, reflecting the sensations or images provided to him.

Every conscious or unconscious isolation of the central sensory power opens the way to the manifestation of the potentiality of reflection of the images that surround you and come from other people or things. The psychical power of a subject increases if exercised, just as exercise works to develop muscles.

Occult science, which has been transformed into the religious esotericism of Christianity, gives you a simple method: it says to the faithful, "Meditate, and you will hear Christ speak."

Scientists laugh when they hear of the practices of Christianity, and what is unfortunately true is that many priests do not believe in or understand what they do; but when the priest at the altar says *Verbum caro factum est,** he does not know or understand that it is a work of accomplished magic; the word has become action and deed through the manifestation of Christ.

Pray, isolate yourselves, meditate, says the Christian, and the Holy Spirit of God will descend upon you. This Holy Spirit of the Christians is the old *telema,* the link between the invisible and the perceptible. But if the spiritualist sits at a table with a sheet of paper in front of him and a pen in his hand and prays, according to Allan Kardec's formula, "Almighty God, let my guardian angel answer me . . . or let the spirit of (whoever it may be) speak to me . . . ," the process is the same. *The freedom of the central intellective power is achieved by relaxing the physical sensibility in man.*

---

*[The Word became flesh. —*Trans.*]

The explanation is the same for all other methods used in divination of all kinds.

The vision in the water (recently called Cagliostro's mirror) or the vision in concave mirrors or on polished surfaces only makes use of the irradiation of light rays reflected by the surface, shining for the physical eye of Pupilla* to determine the movement or action of the secret visual equipment in the human organism.

Music, harmonic or melodic, has the power to act by reflection on the hearer's psyche; in fact, the ordinary auditory apparatus, seized by the vortex of the progression of the notes, or stunned by the vibrations of the metallic instruments, can even produce a state of cataleptic hypnosis in some sensitive subjects.

To recap, in order to go further: the practical means of obtaining the intuition of ultrahuman truth comes down to one: *to make animal senses dormant in order to give complete freedom to the other, the sense which is the conductive medium between the ultrahuman and the human.*

The separating [*separando*]† is the enigma of the great magicians' magic and is the only absolute aim. It is impossible to perceive the intellectual phenomenon without achieving the *detachment,* the *separation. . . .* See how poor our language is! I am using two words which by themselves are improper and have no meaning, because they are taken from the world of things and in (*unitary*) occult philosophy there can be, strictly speaking, neither detachment nor separation.

However, both in matter and spirit, eternally mingled in an astonishing embrace, there are two polarities, and consequently two sensibilities, the finer of which derives from the negation of the coarser, and vice versa.

In this conflict, the equilibrium of the mean term is determined

---

*Cagliostro called Pupilla "the maid who looked into the bottle of water."

†[By *separando,* the Italian Hermeticists mean the separation of the lunar body (including the mercurial and solar bodies), called *separando lunare,* from the physical body through alchemical procedures. There can also be a *separando mercuriale,* which represents the separation of the mercurial and solar bodies from the lunar and physical. —*Trans.*]

within the relativity of life, the *Hermetic or integral magnetism* that is the magical instrument par excellence, because it makes possible understanding of the sensory forces, in their entirety or separately, in the two extremes: a phenomenon that is not possible for the sensists of base matter, nor for the spiritualists who concentrate all higher intellectual psychodynamics toward the extreme pole of the most subtle sensibility.

I feel this explanation is not fully satisfactory in rendering the concept of Hermetic initiation for two reasons: the lack of new words, which I cannot invent, since most people have no idea of the thing, and the error of profane philosophical education that renders the reader incapable of analyzing the dynamic causes of any action of human intelligence in relation to the lowest of sensible creations.

This apparently abstruse discussion will remain so for all those who do not intend to practice but only to talk about it. By *practicing* I mean the difficult training, which leads to the perception of the sensibility, which becomes light and intellective spirit in the mysterious obscurity of the origin of each of us.

To write and speak of magic does not mean to be a magician: a magician is created through a continual process of self-creation, first through the determination of the closest analysis of sensuality and feeling without the preconceptions of asceticism and mechanical materialism, and then through the initiation into the arcanum.

All men and women, as soon as they begin the development of their inner sense or subtle perception, whatever means they use, are only turning back all that is external inertia for the benefit of their psychical development. This world beyond, this world of beings who have already lived or who have not lived an earthly life, cannot be apprehended or judged by the ordinary methods for control of animal senses, and it is useless to try to make believers in this world of those who have not developed the special property that is the eye of the soul, which we have called the sixth sense or subtle perception or telema or intellectual Mercury.

When using the sixth sense, if the test method cannot be controlled by common men, the test or check can always be done physically. A gentleman welcomes you with nice words and manners, and you intuit, you feel through the acute perception of your soul, that he is not sincere: your perception, the feeling you read deep in his soul cannot be tested in itself; the trial method is a certainty for you, but for the others is of dubious worth. But you ask for a test after which nobody can deny the intuition you felt yesterday. You wait a few days: on the first occasion when that man might have been well-disposed toward you, he shows himself for what he is. Your previous intuition has been proved by a physical test.

The same happens in experimental matters of magical occultism.

Faith is blind. *I believe because I am not able to judge.* The ignorant man at the doctor's must have faith in the doctor: I believe, O physician, in your human knowledge. The intelligent man who cannot measure and embrace the Central Unity, Creator and Motion and Life, which is the Great All, must have faith in God. But when we talk of true science, what most people call faith is only *the intuition of a truth through the sixth sense that is waiting to be openly tested in a physical way.*

Without this perception, which is erroneously taken for faith by the vulgar masses, Archimedes would not have discovered the laws of the displacement of water, nor would Galileo have discovered the law of the pendulum, nor would Columbus have discovered America, nor would Darwin have written *On the Origin of Species.*

Read the history of the great alchemists; they spent fifty, sixty, and even more years blowing on their fires to liquefy metals: chemical combinations came one after the other but metals were not vivified nor were they changed into gold. Those who came to possess the law of transformation into the *protogenerating unity* could not say, "I had faith and succeeded" but rather, "The intuition, the perception that I would get there made me keep on in spite of the mocking laughter of the others—and I succeeded."

Now, the *other world* in question, being an assembly of *intelligences, creations, and forces,* can and must be perceived intuitively by those who are psychically advanced, but the certainty of the existence of this world containing intelligences, creatures, and forces must be felt by all men on account of the material effects it produces.

Every action has a reaction, both in the world of mechanical forces and in the hyperphysical world. Now, in the forces, creatures, and intelligences that populate the invisible world, the *action* is the work of the one who has an intuition, or better, by the one who has developed the sixth sense, feeling the presence and the action of hyperphysical forces and intelligences, whose *reaction* has a strong impact on the physical world.

If *a* is the action of extra-human forces and intelligences, which a sensitive person *S* perceives, the reaction *r* is in the realm of the physical.

Astronomically, it is like this:

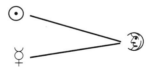

Therefore, in order to avoid any misunderstanding, I mean that if the perception of the action of the other world on the sensible world is exclusively for the one who can subtly perceive the movement of these forces and intelligences, all those who do not rise above mediocrity have the right to have physical proof of these intuitions of the other world from their *sensory reactions*.

Proposition 6—The conflict between religion and science is defined by the sophism of the definition of God and of the Spirit of God.

In magic, in order to understand what we mean by *intelligence,* we should briefly examine the *forces* in nature. I advise my religious readers that in this section I have no intention of putting down the God of any faith; rather I want to erect a temple of reason to the *One* who, transformed by all religious and sectarian controversy, has become a figure of fun to scientists and outside observers.

All definitions are conventional—but light, sound, heat, are forces or manifestations of one force: define the force . . .

So, what is *force?* No more than the soul of any phenomenal production. But the conception of this *single force* cannot be grasped by the human intellect. Wherever we turn we have the intuition of myriad *simple forces in a continual unfolding and manifestation of phenomena.*

The *Single Force* is the life of the universe: the various active *forces* of all manifestations are the life of things, of metals, minerals, vegetable growth, men, and beasts.

The *Single Force* in continual unfolding of itself is Motion; the simple forces are ways of being of *motion or central motion.*

This simple philosophy of things is as old as the hills. Zoroaster venerated the sun, just as Dr. Kremmerz did at the beginning of *Il Mondo Secreto* in 1898. People of no account say that Zoroaster venerated the largest planet because he adored it as the visible God; however, if we studied the mythologies of the sacred East, this concept of the *Single Force and Motion* would be found in all the astronomical religions of antiquity. The sun, ⊙, with its circular form, represents rapid rotation and with its *apparent movement, uninterrupted Motion.* Wherever you see, in the religious symbolism from the ancient Persians to the Egyptians and from Pagans to Catholics, circles, wheels, and round symbols, you can say it is the personification of central motion or the life of the universe that the faithful are being reminded of. The heavenly planisphere of the ancient Egyptians is similar to the wheels of Phoebus's chariot in pagan mythology; the Host, which the Catholics bring forth for the devotion of the faithful, is Zoroaster's and Dr. Kremmerz's sun, which churchly religion keeps in a silver and gold container with rays like the sun that is worshiped by the faithful.

The manifestations of the Single Force or Motion are specific forces.

They are all *physical or natural* forces, and yet we usually divide the physical from the mechanical, from the chemical, from the vegetable, and from the vital.

Above all these varieties and subspecies we place the Force of thought and will, the *psyche* or *nous* of the Greeks, the *neshamah* of the Hebrew Kabbalah, the *mens* of the Latins.

At this point the *Force,* or *Single Motion,* fuses with a principle of Absolute Reason, which represents the reason of this one force, that is, the thinking soul of this life or physical soul of the universe.

In other words, if F represents the Single Central Force, and F^1, F^2, F^3, F^4, and so on, the specific forces of different manifestations, the rough mechanism of these evolutions and manifestations of F remains rough hypothetically because when you ascend from the life of minerals to the life of beings of a superior order, you notice that each phenomenon of force and will is accompanied by another inexplicable conjunct, which in the form of *reason,* of *free choice,* of *equilibrium,* of *idea,* or of *number* determines its quicker or slower manifestation in one way or another.

So this $F,$ or Single Central Force, by itself is only hypothetically blind but, in practice, we notice that it is constantly governed by a law, which is the expression of its reason, which determines its functions. Once this force F reaches the level of a reasonable and evolved man, his psyche, will, or free choice can modify it or, better, can stimulate it, for good or evil, adapt it, in certain proportions, to his requirements for vital force, misuse it against his fellow men, or increase it. But in the phenomena of manifestation of this F in the general, constant, or evolutionary order of nature (one or more men's minds being unable to regulate it), we must perforce suppose that either the Single Force F is by itself capable of organization and thought, or there exists a *mind* at the nth power of the human mind. The progression of intuition expands the creative mind, and where we read about the God who created man, it is God whom man creates in the image and progress of his own mind to manifest himself in all the things that are beyond his powers.

Thus, the ignorant man's God is wretched, petty, and ignorant; and thus, the great God of advanced and refined minds is wonderful. Step-by-step as man progresses, his horizons become wider; the nearer he comes to the indefinable infinite, the more wonderful he finds the Unknown, which escapes him and looms larger as humanity progresses.

The religions, which do not evolve at the same rhythm as the intellectual progress of peoples, are doomed to die or to change; that is why the Christian religion called itself catholic or universal because it was never to find itself in the rearguard of intellectual developments concerning the scientific progress of the faithful; thus, the fierce disagreement between a church, which defends its doctrine badly, and the people who are keen to know and who despise stasis, which in the soul of peoples is the negation of *central movement* and synonymous with death and decomposition!

Let us approach things very simply: the God we create for ourselves is a way to reach the limit of our *mind* to a degree far superior to any human power; however, when the creation of a *sovereign mind* has been achieved in us, then we ourselves become the last step on the road of visible perfection.

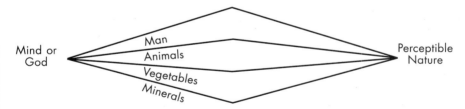

But let us take it further.

From minerals we pass to vegetables; from the latter to animals; and from them to men. But from men to the *One Mind* is a long way, hence the origin of all theologies.

If the force F were brute, the universe would not have an order and a reason in the constant development of all its natural phenomena.

If the force F were by itself reasonable, then not even its lowest part could be subject to man and his mind.

Then, separating

$$F \text{ (Single Force or Motion)}$$

from

$$M \text{ (Universal Governing Mind)}$$

the result is that

$$D \text{ (Concept of God)} = M + F.$$

So, if M stands for the governing stimulus, F must be the resistance: therefore,

$$M + F \ (F^1, F^2, F^3, F^4, \text{ etc.}) = \textit{Realization}; \text{ i.e.,}$$

any phenomenon of any nature and kind, above as below, in matter as in spirit, in the visible as in the invisible, in the perceptible as in the imperceptible, is produced by a governing stimulus (M) *and by the single force or life of the universe.*

In superhuman phenomena m *represents the universal mind; in human-produced phenomena* M *represents the mind of man.*

Let us now come to the conflict between religion and science.

Religious doctrine has pretensions toward defining God, or rather toward defining the indefinable, that is, to make concrete what by its nature cannot be made concrete: the life of the Universe or Force and the Mind, which governs its functions; and against this science and the reason of the reasonable animal rebel.

The Kabbalists, those who can read the hidden and arcane meaning in the Kabbalah, make no pretensions even toward conceiving the idea of God: they understand it as the unknown, inconceivable maker of all phenomena. The manifestation of the *mind* and *force* lies in the production of the phenomena. That is why fire magicians from Isaac to Abraham lit a pile of wood, and while the tongues of flame reached toward heaven and the wood crackled, they worshiped the one who in the consuming flames manifests his power. That is why an obstetrician, when he hears the first cry of a newborn babe, can venerate the *force* and *mind* that perpetuate the animal and human life of a being made in our own image. That is why, when a dying man breathes his last, the most skeptical experimentalist must doff his hat and acknowledge the Life of the universe and the Mind, both of which leave the human carcass to the worms. For the same reason we must bow down to the physical beauty of women, which is the testament of the eternal harmony of nature.

Proposition 7—Intelligence is the most precise expression of the intuition of the Being (Ente).

What I am going to write now is the Gordian knot of the conception of the One God in magic. That is why I recommend the researcher in occult philosophy not to go any further if he has not yet understood the process of investigation of the human mind into the knowledge of the Cause of all Causes.

Force is intuitive, *Motion* is indefinable, and human language also fails to give a precise definition of something, which all men feel in themselves, and which we, in the Latin style, have called Mind (Italian, *mente*).

In everyday grammar, the remnant of an ideal grammar,* the verb or word par excellence is the noun *essere,* "being."† The Latin *ens* is the being (*l'ente*); and the Latin *mens* is a composite of the consonant *m,* indicating possession (a quasi-syncope of *meus*), preceding the noun participle indicating *ens* (being), that is, *Being,* that which exists, which is.

Therefore, let us investigate the hidden meaning of the words: *ente* is the absolute idea of the universal spirit of God; and *mente* (mind) is the word for the relative idea of the universal spirit incarnate and contained in the human body.

The Kabbalists express this name of God in four Hebrew letters,

YOD – HEH – VAU – HEH,

which in magic and magical formulae do not form a name but correspond to the *tetragrammaton,* that is, a "word of four letters" that veils the name of the Universal God rather than revealing it. So they also call

---

*That is, the original grammar of *absolute ideas.*
†[In Italian *essere* means "to be" (verb) and "being" (noun). —*Trans.*]

him the *Ineffable,* which cannot be expressed in words. But if you want to determine the divine spirit incarnate, you have to use five letters, or better, the magical *penta-gramme,* which is symbolized thus:

The pentagram, as can be easily seen, is the image of man with arms and legs outstretched. It corresponds to the five-pointed star, which the Magi who worshiped Christ saw shining in the heavens. This symbol represents universal equilibrium in man: thus, operating magicians consider this talismanic symbol so important, having, as it does, indisputable virtues when traced by masters with the proper rites at the most propitious time.

ENTE (being)	MENTE (mind)
4 letters	5 letters

Intelligence is the effort of the Mind (*mente*) of conceiving, assimilating its virtues, the Being (*ente*) from which it originates—*intelligo* (Latin) is almost *in te lego* (in you I read), from which comes *intellectus,* which the Neoplatonists frequently used in the harmonious Italian language, and which in Dante is used in exactly this sense.

Now:

(a) God cannot be defined
(b) the graphic description of God kabbalistically is a tetragrammaton, a name of four letters, a yod, a heh, a vau, and a second heh

Yod—the active principle of all things, impregnating.
Heh—the passive receiving principle (guttural).

Vau—active impregnation and generation.

Heh—the passive receiving principle.

Therefore, the Hebrew Jehovah, that Jehovah whom ignorant authorities on sacred philosophy have mocked so much, was not a definite thing for Hebrew priests; on the contrary, he was a great and true God containing all the principles of Force, Mind, and Realization, as explained in Proposition 6. The four letters express an eternal law.

A peasant who makes a hole in the ground, plants a seed, and when a season has passed gathers the fruit, carries out all four operations indicated in the Hebrew tetragrammaton:

Yod—the active principle, the peasant digging the hole.

Heh—the earth, or passive element in which the hole is made.

Vau—the fruit-bearing seed.

Heh—the harvest.

This simple operation of the peasant is similar to the operation performed by man in reproducing himself and is similar to any operation in all the realms of nature.

But this is the only plastic conception of the truth of the Hebrew tetragrammaton; if you rise to the heights of the most elevated ideal philosophy, you will find the same unchangeable law.

Now, this kabbalistic sacred name, which perfectly expresses the eternal law of creation, may be differently *understood* according to the psychic development of those who think of this Unity of Mind and Force. Hence came the names of the angels, where archangels or higher intelligences are no more than rays of this central power; so the Catholic religion still has the names of Michael, Raphael, and Gabriel, who are different aspects of the eternal luminous center, or better, they are elevated manifestations of the universal power of Jehovah, the Great God.

Write these names in Hebrew letters; and if you study the Kabbalah well, you will realize that each name is a general law or divine principle.

The idea of these powers and intelligences is not the same for all men, and scientists who take them for curly-headed winged little children are bound to say that the Kabbalists are impostors: do not slander things and people you have never known.

• ◆ •

Now let us ask the question again: *Is there another world of intelligences, of spirits of the dead, and invisible creatures?*

The answer cannot be in doubt after all we have said. This world, which is dubiously hinted at, exists:

1. Because a *Mind* exists whose manifestation is the law of nature.
2. Because *to create means to give form,* and the nothing, the negation of being, is inconceivable and nonexistent.
3. Because the human mind, the image of the Universal Mind, follows the law of all existing things in nature, frees itself of all heavy parts, and evolves seeking contact with the Universal Mind. It would be an exception if its unity, against all laws, fell apart and disappeared on the death of the physical body.

Now, in occultism, or better, in Magic, the work of the magician is twofold: *first, to come, by every means possible (graphic signs, visions, hearing, intuition) into contact with the other world; and second, to move actively in it so as to obtain reactions and effects in everyday real life.*

All this is not done when you are sleeping, hypnotized, or magnetized. It is done in a state of extra-normal exaltation to which none of the three abovementioned states corresponds; rather one's sensibility is highly excited.

In mediumistic manifestations, the medium is passive. In magical operations, the magician is active, and each magician has his own special way of operating and exciting his sensibility—but certainly not by sleeping.

It is not self-hypnosis, nor is it religious ecstasy; modern language does not have a word to express that state. The operator falls into a particular ecstasy in which he does not only undergo the manifestations but governs them, giving them force.

Man must strive with all his might to integrate the powers and virtues of his latent, sleepy, forgetful personality in the face of the new personality imposed upon him by the society in which he lives.

He must not be mystic through excess of spirit, or beast through the preponderance of the grosser of his parts. Thus, slowly evolving, he enters the sphere of *mag:* a state of being that cannot be understood by those who do not experience it.

Mag is the power of active trance; I do not know how to explain more clearly something that very few can understand: it is the state of automatic, volitive trance, a shadow, in all its manifestations and realizations.

Magic considers the great whole in the synthesis of a huge unity that is the Universe. The Universe, being an incommensurable unity x, is equal in functions (or rather, by analogy) to any organized unity of an inferior order: the human body, for example.

The human body, considered as a synthesis, is an organic unity whose parts are the limbs, the viscera, appendages of all kinds, just as each limb, each appendage, and so on, considered as a unit, is formed of muscles, blood, cells, and so forth. Any movement of a muscle or a limb is related to the organic unity of the human body. Stand a man upright; have him raise one foot such that he is standing on the other; the whole organic unity of the body will feel the effort and the effect: the same is true for any movement or sensation.

Let us consider the unity of the Universe by analogy. The limbs, the viscera, the appendages of this monster, which cannot be comprehended in its synthesis, are the stars, the planets, the sun, the moon, and so forth. Any movement of one of these parts of the unity is related to all the rest, which we can see and perceive, in the same way as the human limbs are related to the unity of the physical body. No one in the world will deny that the sun, rising in the east, makes its beneficial effect felt on all the earth it illumines; that the apparent orbit of the sun marks the passing of seasons; that certain signs of the zodiac bring rain or fine weather.

The objection might be made that, in the human-unity, the human will is not subject to any fixed law in the direction of the movements of its parts, while the universe is subject to mathematical laws in the movement of all its planets, so much so that even the orbits of the furthest comets are established and measured by our astronomers. But this is not true.

Because, in the human body (microcosm) as in the universe (macrocosm), we notice an identical analogy between the fixed laws of predetermined movements and accidental movements of any kind.

For example, the fixed laws:

In man—the circulation of the blood, nutrition by way of ingestion, constant renewal of organic tissues.

In the universe—the movement of the planets, the rotation of our planet, the movement of the stars toward major centers, and the movement of occasional satellites.

Chance movements:

In man—any voluntary or involuntary movement of an organ.
In the universe—thermal variations, atmospheric flux, meteors.

The astronomers can try through their meteorological research to establish approximations or probabilities, but so far nobody has described or determined the constant law that governs the origins and the course of cyclones, storms, hurricanes, rises and falls in temperature, non-prevailing winds, and so forth.

Now, if we relate the two unities, *macrocosm* and *microcosm,* man and the universe, it is logical, strictly scientific, although not always perceptible, that any movement in any part of Creation influences the other part and modifies its conditions. We live on the earth and need not resort to Sirius or the movement of Jupiter's satellites to feel or experience the visible effects; the motions of revolution and rotation of the earth, the solar ecliptic, the motions of the moon, are enough to confirm the most apparent alterations that influence us. These elements are enough to establish that the planetary influence of the ancient astrologers corresponds indisputably to the beneficent or maleficent *action of the planets* on our earthly nature. It is all a matter of simplifying the ancient form and seeking the truth in the astrologers' simplest expression.

The sun in Capricorn has a bad influence.

Only an idiot could laugh at this. The sun in Capricorn is the sign of cold, desolating, freezing December: the Yule log surrounded by ice, the hungry wolf who comes out of his mountain lair in search of prey, and winter, enemy of the poor, comes on; in the cold, the ice, the northern gale; then the sun becomes a small child again on the ecliptic of the year, and for the Catholic Church on the twenty-fifth of December Child Jesus is born. Child Jesus, like the sun, who rises up to heaven in the sign of Aries, at Easter, when the sun reawakens spring on the earth.

Now, as in these apparent cases of the passing of the seasons in the astronomic year, so the influence of the apparent motion of the sun and the waxing and waning of the moon have a more definite and real effect than is ordinarily believed, at times exaggerated, at others minimal, on all the three kingdoms of nature. I will certainly not remind you that the waxing and waning of the moon have an evident influence on crabs, oysters, the impregnation of fish and mollusks; nor that, in the countryside, some phases of the moon are considered unpropitious for pruning; nor that some fevers seem to take on the characteristics of the phases of the moon in a single week; nor that there is a relationship, experimentally proved by Palmieri and his collaborators, between the waxing and waning of the moon and the eruptive phases of volcanoes; but if a genius should come and reveal to the world the laws that govern the relationship between the phases of the moon and the nerve centers of the human body, there would be a great revolution in experimental science and we would find the reason behind certain nervous epidemics, ordinarily attributed to the circumstances of the times, and the reason behind so many of the mysteries in the cure of ordinary diseases, that in one planetary period take on a benign form or a malignant tendency while they disappear in another.

Having said this, for the sake of clarity, I advise beginners to choose carefully the period in which to begin their work.

I advise the period of the waxing moon and, most of all, the lunations in November and December, or better yet, the two signs of Scorpio and Capricorn, so as to try the first operations under Aries (April) and the more difficult ones in Virgo,* to reach balance in Libra.

With a serene mind let us turn our aspirations upward.

1. Cultivate your own mind so that it can, after having risen, first perceive and then know the laws of our own physical and spiritual nature.

2. Work toward perfection in yourself so that the nature of the

---

*"Thou knowest well, my son, that you are the son of Virgo (Virgin), and if Virgo thou violatest, thou killest the seed of thy people and becomest an incestuous parricide, and so thy brain will burn; but if Mercury thou canst draw with Virgo the Glorious, placing the crescent moon under her feet, thou, in thy turn, will become the father of demigods. For if thou canst unite, with Ariadne's ancient thread, the water of Orion and the white Mercury of Virgo's moon, and canst keep off the fiery Mars, thine eyes will see sights never seen before and thou wilt harvest miracles with the scythed moon turned toward the earth. So, if thou dost recognize me as they father, thou must succeed in tearing the secret from me, driving the cane of thy insufflation away from Moses's and Aaron's rod, which is my rod, and keep thyself one, if thou dost not want me to destroy thee through my generosity. Here thou wilt see the Saturnian secret, which is the gift of life and death, of love, of generation and plenty, and thou must not forget that in Virgo thou, using the methods of our art, shall prepare the *rod* [*la verga*], as thy master teacheth thee, with no knot, and cleanly cut with the scythe in the form of a consecrated crescent; without Virgo's rod [*verga di virgine*] thou canst not become a magician; thou must not misunderstand me or thou wilt sow your Mercury in the sand, nor expect me to write more clearly; thou must ask thy guide for the intelligence of this." (From my book, *Delle Stelle e dei Soli* [Of Stars and Suns]).

beast, while we are still alive on earth, be conquered by spiritual supremacy.

3. Enter into rapport with the invisible beings around you, dominate the bad and the inferior, and learn from the more perfect, to get closer to the supreme truth.

4. Penetrate the laws that govern each earthly realization, and *use them when it is right to do so*—to help your fellow men.

5. Prepare the spiritual progress of mankind with all your might, because as the spirituality of men progresses so civilization proceeds, since civilization means realization of the spirituality of the masses.

6. Strengthen bonds of brotherhood between men, and by solving the problem of souls, solve the social problem of peoples.

This is the scientific and humanitarian credo of occultism, but it is not a program for *one life,* but for centuries; it is the program of the priesthood of science. A modest man of good will, a small cog in the big wheel of mankind, does what little he can in all humility, and will start to realize that part of the great ideal which he feels most congenial to his self.

•◆•

Every fluidic organism and every spirit living in the man, made of flesh, cartilage, and bone, has limits to its development; just like any body, taken physically, has limits to its action in the perceptible world.

I will explain using this example: all able-bodied men can live the human life, but one can become an athlete with the powers of Milo of Croton and another, with all the will in the world, cannot lift an iron bar that weighs one hundred pounds. This shows that an *individual,* studied from the physical and intellectual point of view, comes into the physical world with qualities peculiar to his embodiment. This represents all that is called the *destiny* of a man.

I recommend my learned readers to study this problem deeply and to come to a precise idea of it, because there is nothing that puts such a damper on illusions as this consideration of man in his physical and intellectual reality.

We must distinguish all the factors that are part of the formation of a man who acts in the human comedy:

(a) *Physical heredity* (which is one of the achievements of modern science but which the ancients knew and studied all the same; conquest of a truth that will never again be modified, simply because it is a truth).

(b) *Climatic and astrological circumstances* (official science does not admit any influence of the moment of birth on the subsequent course of the physical life of the individual, but it will soon realize that it must take the influence of these moments on men into consideration, in the same way as zoological philosophy had to accept as necessary the influence of climate on races).

(c) *Human education* (education in childhood and youth is a continual process of suggestion that begins in the tenderest years and ends when the young man, matured into life, has become an unconscious machine as a result of the upbringing he has received; Jesus of Nazareth said: "Never hit a child, because hitting, even with a flower, leaves a deep impression in the tender incarnate spirit"; the child is like uncultivated land where good crops as well as weeds can be sown and bear fruit).

(d) *Will or volitive power* (which is an emanation of the individual's intellective power modified by the human environment in which the individual grows and acts).

(e) *The resistance of the environment to the will of the individual* (which always exists in society as a strong factor, which the individual overcomes through the law of adaptability).

(f) *Perseverance of volitional activity* (which is a modification of the environment under the tenacity of the individual agent's strength of will).

(g) *The intelligence or spirit of intellectual light* (which is always impeded or modified in some aspects in life by the action of the six preceding elements).

Educating and remaking your conscience, stripping it of any influence to which it is subservient—ancient superstitions, environment, habits, deceitful visions, servile imitation of established types—is necessary.

The master key to the educational idea of our personality is to be found in this purification of conscience from the mists of human convention. Only then does the Hermetic novitiate begin to bear his fruit—when the conscience is free to perceive a twofold current:

1. The sensory, or psychic, current, which comes from the periphery.
2. The instinctive current, which begins to strip away the tendencies of the ancient man in us.

"Know thyself" is precisely the initiation to light, the purification from all that is artificial or "sub-created," and which human social ignorance has inflicted upon us. Man has in himself unfathomed depth where (following the reasoning materialist) all impressions, forms, and ideas that our conscience may forget are recorded from birth.

In us there is an ancient part and a very modern one. This ancient part (historic man) is the marrow, the center of the outwardly visible man, reasoning, with a consciousness formed by sensations and by the adaptation of his mentality to the surroundings in which he operates.

The unconscious, the subconscious, the subliminal, belong to that astral field, which is in us (*astral* = black, without light), from which spring forth, every now and then, many disorders and the most inconceivable wonders: the flash of genius and the paroxysm of madness.

Identify this field as a core, an entity, a person, and there you will find a historic unity of your spirit throughout all your past lives. The scientific word for this historic individual, who is our solar soul, shrouded in a cloud of black mist, has not yet been invented, because the historic personality in us is not only soul or spirit or pure breath but a whole of special activity, which comes to our consciousness as living and vegetating men, like the prompter for the characters in a comedy, in the most critical moments of forgetfulness and impotence.

In the simple symbology of the Kabbalists, the upright triangle (*A*) is the apparent, conscious, visible, and perceptible life; the man who lives in the full consciousness of external reason, the man with his head held high, above the level of the earth (*A'*). If the triangle is turned upside down (*B*), like a wedge stuck deep in the earth below the level of the earth (*A"*), it represents the mysterious occult life, in the unfathomable darkness of the death of man; the vital man in his unconscious, the misty, dark, deep astral field, which does not belong to the outward, visible life:

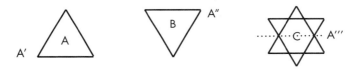

The double triangle, that is, the penetration of the two (*C*), such that the level (*A'''*) is fixed at the middle intersection of the sides of the triangles, is the magician, a man integrated between apparent external consciousness (upright triangle) and the occult part of his consciousness (inverted triangle), which stands in place of the occult God with all his powers.

The unconscious and its intentions manifest themselves through spontaneous actions, shooting out without conscious and volitive control. Freud uses the two words *interference* and *intention:* therefore, he attributes to this internal area, which reveals itself through slips and surprises, intentions, which are volitive actions, and gives the unconscious (astral field) not only the capacity to retain images and impressions but also an *aeonian* power, that is, a personality capable of conceiving the same acts as our conscious personality.

This is not Freud's conclusion, but mine; from the point of view of magical philosophy, the consideration of impressive powers, of a second complete personality represents the stumbling block for all philosophies.

The internal man is the father (*qui es, eris, fuisti* [who you are, you shall be, you were]), the conscious man, the inhibitor: who, through his education, and the ideas inculcated in him, and from the milieu in which he lives and his respect for civil, moral, penal, and religious laws, suppresses any manifestation of the historic personality, as soon as that personality diverges from the life conforming to the reactions of the external and conscious character.

This censorious obstacle, be it preexisting or recent, is a huge bridge that deters the common man from the attempts in magical experiments, since the obstacle is not only spiritual in the common sense of the word but has power over all physical and mental life, influencing success in practical life as a reasoning inhibitory power, at times instinctive, more often marked by sentimentality, with one hundred different faces, and imitative in origin.

I consider this theory of Freud only in relation to the psychology of the researchers in magic and of the practitioners of the orders or brotherhoods of Isis, and I must separate the psychoanalytic concepts from other elements of our practice, even admitting that psychoanalysis encroaches upon the field of our philosophy and carries elements of the latter into the scientific field.

Fui, sum, ero [I was, I am, I shall be].

If, when you find yourself on the edge of the deep astral abyss, you ask who your God is, the Voice answers you:

I am the one who was, is, and evermore shall be. Death did not change me, any more than the dispersed ashes of my corpse that was has reduced the power of my being.

An ancient initiate asked the voice that told him the truth, "Who are you?"

And it answered in the teaching of Pythagorean mathematics, which can be translated thus:

I am in you, and for you. I am not you (that is, your mind). You have prayed, that is, in the form of prayers you have impregnated the invisible beloved. I, the voice who speaks to you, am the fruit of your act, I am the Mercury of your intellect."

Osiris acts upon Isis; Horus is born. Three is the ternary, it is Mercury, it is the fruit, the product of the first binary.

The first problem, which faces the initiate, to this integral science is to ask his Hermetic light, whose source no man knows, "Who are you who manifest yourself, bringing me truth?"

Some say, "It is me, my ingenuity" (*in-genius,* the genius in me).

Some say, "It is an angel" (*angelus* = messenger).

Some say, "It is a daimon or a god."

If he does not understand the law so simply expressed in the Kabbalah, he will never understand it—like the inspired mystics of religious forms of all kinds.

Well, that voice, essentially Hermetic in nature, should answer:

I am not you, but I am not a stranger to you.

I am in you for your sake, and I am not you.

The unknown wise man is approaching.

Hermes is the Greek name for the Latin Mercury. Nebo, Hermes, Mercury, Lucifer, Holy Spirit, are synonyms for the same state of being of human intelligence whose secret laws are still forbidden to men. It is this intelligence, which is changed from light into force and produces the forms of magic that tend to be objective, from magnetism to the projection of psychic forces, to the different forms of mediumism, and throughout those phenomena in which an ungraspable intelligence watches, and which one man considers the spirit of the dead, another a demon, and still others an angel.

What is most important is that Hermes manifests himself, since the Light of Hermes will lead you to integration, because you will begin to see the external and internal worlds in a way and with a feeling that is different from the way you saw it yesterday.

Hermes must bring us to an understanding of mental motion outside of any place, surface, or point.

Man can, through the analysis of his mind or mental motion in its dimensionless space, join with the universal mind-motion—which must fill the same space—and draw upon its thoughts and knowledge.

If you conceive the dimensionless space of mental motion and the motion outside of any place, then time, in the operations of the mind, does not exist.

The human mind (if you Hermetically penetrate this function) identifies itself with a universal mind outside of time, drawing from it a divine virtue that changes into miraculous powers, although they are miracles only for the masses who ignore the universal law.

•–◆–•

The standard examination of the elements that go to make up man, the ternary of *intelligence, physical body,* and *sidereal* or *astral body* or *peri-spirit,* is synthetic, but the examination must go further, so that also those who are followers of elementary spiritualism, through the simple light of reason, may understand that the three terms of spirit, peri-spirit, and physical body are harmoniously related to each other.

Harmony is the correct proportion of relativity between the trinitary elements making up the synthesis that is *man:* in fact, *as the circumference is proportional to the radius,* as the contents are proportional to the container, so the peri-spirit is not relative but *harmonizes* with the physical body and the spirit. Because between the physical body, the astral body, and the spirit only harmony exists, a constant and varying proportion in the reciprocity of the terms, as in music, where the harmony and sound are obtained through the various components of the overall sound, each of which is at times predominant, at times silent. Music is the most exact expression of the harmony of the three elements that constitute man; the harmony of sounds is the expression, established as a law, of their reciprocity.

One can observe in practice that the necessity for man to adapt himself to his living environment develops, in greater or lesser proportion, his spirit, his peri-spirit, and his physical body. In a society of gladiators, the physical body predominates; in a society of intellectuals, the spirit dominates; and the sidereal body represents the connecting link between one and the other, and it follows somehow in its development the law of compression of resilient bodies that absorb the shock of a collision between two opposed forces. From another point of view, it acquires the tensile properties of the elastic bodies that, although allowing the distancing between two extreme factors (spirit and matter), preserves the power of reuniting them as soon as they come back to the state of inertia.

The analysis of the functions of the sidereal or astral body is long and difficult, and in order to understand its entire essence one must be greatly advanced in the production of the phenomena of natural magic and in the development of one's astrality. I cite the case of *materializations.* Even the people who have studied in particular the materializations achieved through mediums repeat a *commonplace* of spiritual philosophy: that each materialization is an exteriorization of the astral body; in fact, this is not so, because *there is no materialization without the contribution of both the spirit and the physical body, and only the projection outward belongs to the peri-spirit.*

I am aware that this statement upsets all the received ideas of many spiritualists, *but it is so* in the practice of natural magic; if it were not so, the materialized apparitions would not remove weight and strength from the cataleptic mediums, nor would they feel tired, when they reawake, from exhaustion of the physical body, which feels the need to recover the lost strength. In the spells of black magic (*enchantments, evil spells, acts of sorcery*) a part of the peri-spirit is not expelled from the body to be attached to the *objects involved,* but the sentiment of love or hate is materialized through the exteriorization and fixing of magnetism in the physical body, under the action of the spirit over the sidereal body, which in the magician, through the masculine action of the inspiring intellect, operates like a feminine element in the realization of the active conception and the plastic nutrition of the concrete fact; that is why the ancient schools in magic used the word *androgynous* to mean that in each magical operation there was a real process of generative *incubation,* whose mechanism is perceived through practice, and which in the third part of this work we will be in a position to study deeply when we examine the doctrines known thus far on the polarity of fluidifications.

Going back to our procedure of the analysis of man, we must realize every day that the instinctive or fatal aim of man is corrected by *necessity*—just as a projectile or a bullet expelled from a gun is deviated or stopped in its trajectory by an obstacle.

The man who is free of himself acts according to the intelligent primal action that placed him among the living; the *necessity* that opposes him is the physical and moral environment in which his human life plays out, so the necessity to conform to the environment, or means of existence, develops the *faculties* of one of the three factors more than the other two.

Consequently, this resistance of the environment to the activity of the virgin individual according to his nature must be seriously considered in the analysis of the individual, dividing it into the factors indistinctly acting upon his trinitary constitution.

So, if we call:

A, the spirit;
B, the peri-spirit;
C, the physical body;

we can make an equation:

$$A + B + C = a + b + c + d + e + f = Man.$$

Now, given the absolute constitution of the individual is $A + B + C$, in the practical explanation his power of realization is relative to all the factors $a + b + c + d + e + f$ that we have studied as coefficients of the power of life.

Two men, born of the same father and mother (factor a), in the same month and country (factor b), vary in their human education (factor c): the one can develop his physique more, the other one his intellect;

the one may not have developed his will in an environment that is continually hostile, the other may be so strong and powerful as to modify the environment according to his will (factors *d, e, f*); the one uses his intelligent activity in one way, the other in another way.

•◆•

Now, there is a larval element that acts on the mind of every man, and it is the fantastic dream of each; it has a nature similar to that of fantastic pride: the vain long for the greatest honors, the libidinous for subjugating every beautiful woman to their powerful masculine pride, the miserly covet money; only the enlightened look for truth alone, above all honors, women, and wealth.

If you make use of the law, you will have everything; but do not wish for everything through the law or by bending the law to your own ends; otherwise not only will you not reach your aim but you will also bring all hell down around your ears if you wish for things that the just gods will deny you.

Divine magic considers the truth *one,* the light *one,* God *one,* matter *one,* the Universe *one,* the force *one.*

The way of perceiving this *Single Intelligent Force* must be the same for all initiates, as it is one in its synthetic essence of being and one in its perception, and when an initiate studies and progresses in Naples he must feel and see this *single truth* and its laws in the same way as another who studies and progresses in Copenhagen, Melbourne, or Lima.

This unity of vision concerning the hidden God and his laws forms the universal brotherhood of initiates and the unity of all the classical religions, from the most ancient to the most recent.

This unity of all truths in the *single truth* inevitably brings profane science to discover the real truth of things and to form the theocracy of scientists.

The initiates of all the world are brothers because they all perceive the truth in the same way and with the same laws: two of them meet and recognize each other because they understand each other.

It is not so for the mediums of spiritualism or the seers of schismatic religious movements; each of them sees and hears that *particular spirit of things, which is not the universal spirit of God.*

Apollo spoke in the same way in all his oracles, and the Greek fable of Apollo who defeated the serpent Python is a magic legend because the ☉ center of light (Apollo) dominated the spirit of earthly mud, which is the Astral Serpent of magic, and which corresponds to the serpent that Catholic statuary places at the feet of the Virgin Mary, wound around the horns of the moon.

For the magicians the serpent Python is what we must dominate; for the spiritualists, on the other hand, it is what they must listen to. If you abandon yourself to the coils of the serpent you will become prophets of the astral, prey to all psychical illusions; you are caught in the whirling vortex of all the impressions, of all the images making up the cinema of the soul of the earth.

In this vortex, in this current of low earthly breath, everything is mixed with mud. Spiritualism plays with it. Its communications are only the *aura* of the times in which the spirits write and manifest themselves, and you can even find disembodied spirits who use scientific language, like those at Salpêtrière, in speaking of truth and absolute science.

The Magic of the magicians, as in the emblem of Cagliostro, a serpent transfixed by an arrow, aims at the sun ☉ passing above the dragon, that horrible dragon that is the terrible guardian of Real Truth. The legends of Jason, Bellerophon, Perseus, Theseus, are different fables about the same conquest of truth. The fantastic battles in Nordic mythologies between knights and dragons, between generous and valiant defenders of truth and monsters who belched fire and swallowed up peoples, are simply similar artificial representations of this truth.

You will never be an initiate if you continue to play about with your astral serpent, which is earthly in all its manifestations, even in its language, which reveals, in all vacuous and academic spiritual communications, the human grammatical form which is the expression of *the relative ideas of the earth and its children.*

•—•

Dear reader, at this point I will touch on a question of divine philosophy, about which those who know cannot tell everything and those who do not know, but think about it, remain perplexed. *Is the language of truth human? Can it be rapidly translated into human language?*

Is the language the spirits use to talk to mediums the language of spirits?

If, on the contrary, it is the psychical translation made by mediums, is it a faithful and uniform translation of the spirits' ideas?

In magic, the language of causes is a part reserved for the masters. *Divine ideography* is the key to all religious symbolism and the secret of talismans, of sacred hieroglyphs, of occult books. This key is won from the invisible, through a continuous communication of our ego with the world of causes, as soon as the terrible serpent dies, transfixed by the initiate's willpower. You will get the key from Saint Peter the apostle at the gate of mystical paradise, if you are a Christian; or Isis, stretching out her white and elegant hand, will let you touch it if you prefer to enter the Egyptian garden; in any case, only then will you have a complete knowledge of signs and of the power of characters both in divine and natural magic, and only when your virtue has made you deserving will you know how to use them and what they correspond to.

For now these few words will suffice to warn mediums that they will never again hear the language of God if they keep on listening hour after hour, day after day, to the enticing song of the serpent's creatures—they will never go beyond the known world.

I said: *Don't listen to any communication; you can interpret only lucid dreams, and never literally.*

In this connection I think I have clearly said that the serpent speaks the language of men, and God the language of God.

Operations in magic are of two minds: one implies communication with the soul of the universe; the other determines the domination of the astral serpent, or soul of the earth.

Operations of the former kind put man (the one who by working, initiates himself) in relation to the *Universal Spirit*. He who begins is, like all men, like all things, imbued and soaked through with the earthly aura. He doesn't know—since he knows no concrete things—even how to forge his will to pass through the vortex and penetrate the world of causes. The first operations give him two things: the spur to seek the new ether and the strength to succeed.

When the operation has this rule, or magic ideal, it is no longer a religious practice because *even if the beginners carry it out through faith alone, it is only a calculation of transcendental philosophy;* it is consequently essentially scientific, and not unworthy of any doctor.

Those who start well will soon have glimpses of divine light, not because the angels will come down from heaven and carry the beginner out of the earthly stream, but because the spirit of God, which is in him, will little by little free him from all earthly shackles, till he becomes a prophet. As he progresses and raises himself, he enters into communication with the spirit of the master, who, beyond the barrier of the Dragon, waits for those who get there and enters into direct relation with their spirits.

Those who think they are suited to the trial must not and cannot underestimate such a high ideal, included in a practice that is scientific, that is, wise and not blind superstition.

A *prayer* is an act of concrete fluidification of one's will. To formulate an idea and wish for its realization is a prayer. Since my readers need no prayer books, they are warned that if they aspire to spiritual ascent their ideas must be very clearly formed in their minds—and they will soon get results—because such clearly formed ideas pass through the astral aura of the earth and are gathered by the cupbearer beside the throne of the *Sun*—to whom, at the beginning of this book, I addressed a prayer thus:

> *O Sun,* you who sweep the darkness of the great night of passionate phantoms, of the ghosts of the most uncontrolled desires, of the

proud creations of human arrogance, illumine the ignorance of the one who, purged of the influences of the voluptuousness of temporal things, is thirsty for the eternal truths—and let the idolater of the Beast, bound to the vainglory of ignorance, feel your divine ray and prepare himself for the advent of Christ.

That *Sun,* whom I addressed at the time, is the Sun whom all operators must address: whether you call it Sun, or *God,* or *Universe,* or *Single Force,* or *First Principle,* or *Tetragrammaton,* or *Universal Kingdom,* it is the kingdom of Light you invoke and to whom you address yourself.

The Holy Spirit, the dove messenger of light, is the ray of the Sun shining in your soul. This soul, if it changes into a dove, might make a marriage beyond the limits of known actions.

I warn all inconstant men and women to go on playing about with the rules of spiritualism and never to attempt the concrete operations in magic, because they run a great risk.

I will explain the risk in theory: the initiation into magic is a wrestling match with the Dragon of the astral stream. As in all struggles, one can win or lose—but in this struggle one either wins or dies.

As long as you live the common life, the Serpent will protect you and sleep; but as soon as you try to go beyond its limits, the Serpent awakens and hisses sharply, squeezes you and restrains you. Steadfast men and women of faith defeat it; the madmen who tease it without force and will, end by being eaten, *because in all magic the interruption of any operation before its completion brings about a terrible reaction, whose effect is exactly opposite to that which the operator aims for.*

All operations in magic have two periods, one of reaction and the other of action: the former period is negative, the latter positive. It almost always happens that the novice, seeing the contrary effect occurring, stops, frightened, and there is a complete mess. On the contrary, through resistance, insistence, coercion, the operator's efforts are rewarded by positive results. The grave of all ideals is inconstancy, and I have seen terrible and frightful examples of it.

Don't attempt initiation with a light heart, or with the nonsense of so-called *common sense*. In magic, you must knock assiduously and not stop halfway. Those who fall, even if they find their master again, will have to start again from the beginning, but if they don't find their master again, the only thing to do is to ask for God's forgiveness for having allowed themselves to be blinded by passions, by the false logic of fear and mistrust, and for not having understood that, between mistake and truth, they had to choose the least seductive one as a companion for success, though it be the most bitter and repugnant.

If you are anxious to succeed, be always vigilant, constant, and active.

The active spirit of Universal Nature does not give itself, but lets itself be attracted by those who are active. I said that the intelligences or spirits or fluidic natures appear to us like flashes of lightning: well, the only great and powerful lever of the human mind, which connects it to God through the serpent of earthly will, is this zeal or activity proper to the spirits of Mercury. That is why Dante begins the seventh canto of his *Paradise* with this tercet, inexplicable to the profane science of the grammarians:

> *Hosanna sanctus Deus sabaòth,*
> *Superillustrans claritate tua*
> *Felices ignes horum malacòth!*

> [Hosanna, O Thou Holy God of Hosts,
> that with Thy Clarity dost brighter make
> the happy fires of these celestial realms!]*

Activity, intelligent activity alone, can bring about the greatest of conquests to which a man of genius can aspire: the Truth of Causes, which is above stagnant inertia, of which disbelief is a vulgar symptom,

---

*Translated by Courtney Langdon.

and this activity is the means of achieving an ideal that to the common masses is the most poetic of follies.

• ◆ •

Initium is translated in Latin dictionaries as "beginning." But if you read it according to the analytical rules of the temple it means "seed that produces," that is, the principle of activity in nature (both of spirit and matter), and it was of special significance in the mysteries of Ceres, the *natura naturans* of Christian theologians from Saint Thomas Aquinas to Bellarmino.

Initium and *initiation* in the language of the temple means the admission to the temple where the priests of science gathered.

What should be understood by initiation has nothing to do with mysticism.

It is another kind of materialism because, through instruction, it forms and builds operators, officiating priests with a pure touch who speak with the right tone.

We represent a school of rationalism that deals with the spiritual problem, and we are not mystics. Our creed is an exposition of concrete ideas that agree with an efficacious general methodology.

The *neophyte* is the one who aspires.

In the Mosaic religion of the Hebrews and in Essenism, he was called a *Levite*. In monasticism he is called a *novice*.

This *neophyte,* before entering the temple, before passing the threshold to attempt the conquest of its uncommunicable mysteries, was subjected to terrible trials, descriptions of which my readers can find in all books dealing with initiation. In other words, the custodian of the temple opened the door to the mysteries only to the neophyte who could be trusted to ascend on account of his virtues and perseverance.

In the Egyptian lodges, the neophyte enters, pushing the door of the synedrion where the first-degree masters are sitting around the flaming fire, dressed in red, masked, their heads wrapped in priestly swathes. When the neophyte opens the door, all the masters run to him, surround him, and hold their daggers to his throat, calling him traitor and violator of the unrevealable secret of nature. Then they consult about how to kill him, to sacrifice his spirit to the gods who protect their order, they set up a court and condemn him to death by fire. Then they go into a large enclosure where a pyre is lit. Two of the masters undress the traitor and throw his clothes on the fire, and they go as far as to scorch the flesh of the condemned man with flames. When the hierophant, or grand master, comes and defers the execution, he delivers to the neophyte, naked in front of the flaming fire, a speech more or less like this:

You were so bold as to violate the door that keeps the mysteries of truth from the vulgar of the living, and this proves that you are either a man of courage or a rash fool. I can judge you because I can read in your soul and I judge your daring as reckless folly; you didn't know you were heading for a violator's death. I defer your execution; I put it off, I don't pardon you; if you want to save yourself, you must defeat the fire that consumes you.

"... and the water that chokes you," adds the oldest master.

"... and the air which bears the breath of the earth," adds another.

"... and the earth that swallows up souls," says a third.

Then the hierophant resumes:

If you defeat these four powerful phantoms of the negation of spirit, you will join our family and advance; otherwise your death is put off to the day when you quake.

And no one will be able to rescue you, because the proof of your treason is that unworthily you have violated the entrance to the temple.

Then the hierophant assigns a master to the neophyte, who dresses him in white, and the neophyte swears to keep silent about all that he has seen and will see, and to come through his trial or to die.

The priesthood, organized in a hierarchy, did all this following a ritual or code, which preserved their order from any intrusion or violation. In present-day circles, impure people are not admitted so as to preserve the purity of the others. We see the precedents in ancient times, putting on trial all that a curious man could promise.

When the neophyte was ready, the master came forward, received him, and initiated him; that is, *he cast into him the seed that was to bear fruit.*

From this concept of sowing the fruit-bearing germ in the individual came the sacred expression *in inter-humum;* that is, sown or created for the second time, and that is why in Essene-Christian initiation the master was called father, because the master who initiates is the father of the disciple's spirit. Hence the common syncope of *initium* through analogous assonance and consonance. In the Catholic Church, the confessor is called father.

Now a great misuse is made of the word *initiation,* and everyone thinks it means the beginning of something. *Initiamenta, initiator, initium* are pagan words with two interpretations, one vulgar, the other priestly, and their original use was in the rites of Ceres.

In-itio (*itio, itionis,* the generating movement, the beginning), in the ancient sacred language, corresponded to the breath that Genesis says God Almighty used to infuse his divine spirit into Adam, the man of clay; hence, *initium* is different from *in-itio.*

Ceres, the goddess who could fertilize and be fertilized, could convey with her mysteries the idea that priestly power should cast into the neophyte the seed that brings understanding of hidden things.

In order for you to receive this redemption, which is the work of indispensable preparation, the law tells you:

1. Always live a very pure and austere life.
2. Never appear, nor wish to seem, but be.
3. Always do good, and be guided by the purest justice when doing good.

4. Consider gluttony, lust, and the influence of the profane world as your enemies.

5. Purify yourself after every deed, and think before acting.

6. Say only what you know is true, which you have experienced to be true; don't give what you don't yet possess; don't wish for what your impurity prevents you from obtaining.

7. Speak as little as you can, don't cast pearls before swine, and never lie to yourself.

8. Always be an example of morals and justice, and before violating the law of others think that you don't want others to violate your law.

9. Purify your word through silence, and your body through fasting, and remember that good words, good thoughts, and good actions open the occult kingdom where one thinks and creates, keeps silent and learns.

But let's go back to what I promised: the temple was opened to the neophyte only after his trials, and the *initiation* was the act of entering the temple, receiving from an experienced priest the fruit-bearing seed—that is why, also in our modern language, we call *initiate* he who has gone into the knowledge of mysteries, and *adept* he who has reached a realization of them.

At this point, it is useful to note that initiation to absolute science is neither obtained nor given in the same manner to everybody.

We distinguish:

(a) initiation through rites
(b) initiation through conferral
(c) direct initiation

First, *initiation through rites* is the one I have chosen to establish a school of magic in Italy. The master who gives it must be able to perceive that his disciple has entered into the zone of purification, wherever he is, and at certain moments to communicate with him, or assign him a deputy for himself in the extra-human area.

Second, *initiation through conferral* is the one used by visibly constituted societies, with a hierarchy of degrees, and the power to initiate is thus conferred by a master to his practicing representatives.

Third, *direct initiation,* on the other hand, is the communion a master himself makes directly with a disciple, and in this case it is a true dedication of the master to his disciple. This happens only in the case of an extra-human mandate, which, otherwise, no master *gives himself.*

• ◆ •

To achieve a realization, magic employs all the external means a man can use; in religions also, the pomp of sacred services, priestly garments, the temple ceremonial, are magic. The same thing happens in sects. But if the pomp is magic in religions, the magic of magicians, taken by itself in its essence, needs only one thing to produce miracles: will.

In the great ceremonial of the Catholic religion, the Requiem Mass and the *Te Deum* are real and great collective operations. The priests, led by a senior operator, perform the analogous ritual, and sing and pronounce words, which have a power that depends upon those who sing and pronounce, upon the faith of a congregation, which is present, prays, and takes part in the ceremony.

> *The substance of things hoped for faith must be,*
> *And argument of things invisible,*

says Dante,* but the "argument of things invisible" in the souls of the masses, who are very keen on eternal signs, is roused with the pompous form of priestly rites, and even the soul, which is least touched by ideals, feels moved and is taken into the general motion of souls and overwhelmed by what in these rites is atavistic memory and fear of the unknown.

---

*[*Paradise,* canto XXV (11.64–65, trans. by Dorothy L. Sayers and Barbara Reynolds, (London: Penguin, 1962).—*Trans.*]

Books have been published lately on mass psychology, but *philosophical research,* which ignores psychic force and its contagion, will always be superficial in its consideration of psychology and its paradoxes.

In churches, processions, revolutions, civil ceremonies, the key to the general commotion lies in stimulating the feeling pervading the chain of all the participants' psyches. In a brave army, even those with cowardly souls become courageous, and we need only visit the shrines of the Madonna of Lourdes or the Madonna of Pompeii to study how the most balanced soul feels moved and overcome at times of mass crisis of faith.

In this connection I could write about profound, though simple, things, I could speak of disturbing truths capable of shaking not only the order of religions, but also the order of nations, if those in authority allowed me to let politically passionate, ambitious, and bad men to get hold of the secret of how to become masters of the souls of the reasoning and easily intoxicated mob who are nowadays called by the pompous name of "the sovereign masses"!

It is nevertheless clear that, in the ceremonial magic of religious pomp, faith (if its seed is present) invades all the people, sucking them in like a whirlpool.

It is not so in divine and natural magic practiced by a knowledgeable and capable magician; to the wonderful rituals, rich in sacred and religious accoutrements and trappings, the magician only substitutes his spiritualization with *intelligence* and his fluidification with the *realization* of what he wants,

He thinks or is inspired, finds analogies, and through his art he achieves his end.

Some philosophers, who want to explain everything through hypnosis, say that in fakirism and magic everything is based on the self-hypnosis of the operator; that signs, ciphers, and magic apparatus serve only to put the magician into such states of excitement so as to produce the phenomena.

Others, on the contrary, maintain that the objects used in working magic are charged with human magnetic fluid, so that they work with the magnetism with which they are charged.

The former as well as the latter have based their conclusions on laboratory experiments and have had partial success, but they are all convinced that their own assumptions are true.

Hypnotists ascribe the power of producing phenomena to the projection or liberation of the magician's intelligence or spirit; so they put a subject in a somnambulistic state and order him to produce a given physical phenomenon.

They have only half-succeeded, or they have not succeeded at all, but they have certainly proved, on the outside, that the subjective phenomena have all been produced.

The physician who puts a sensitive subject to sleep and offers him a glass of water, telling him that it is poison, and obliges him to drink, has poisoned that person with drinking water. The same is true, say the hypnotists, for any subjective phenomenon produced by an individual who, like fakirs, can hypnotize himself at will.

But objective phenomena cannot be explained in this way. At this point, magnetizers, with Baron du Potet, author of *Magie Dévoilée* [Magic Unveiled], at their head, come in and say that a clever magnetizer can project his magnetic fluid onto objects and give them a specific force, so that magic potential is made objective. In this way they explain the power of talismans, potions, or any clothing that the operator wears or employs.

Both the former and the latter are mistaken because the secret of working magic is neither the magician's self-hypnosis nor the magnetization of the objects the operator uses.

Let's examine the weak points of the two theories.

Self-hypnosis might carry the exaggeration of subjectivity.

If a man hypnotizes himself, he might believe he is looking at an eagle when he has only a dove in front of him. If a man did so, he would succeed only in voluntarily killing his reason and his spirit. Instead of becoming a magician, he would become a laughingstock.

Magnetism, as a determination of the will, is an incomplete force to be used by itself by an operator, because it can only be projected on things so that they are fortified with intention, but not with *intelligence;* the magician uses magnetism transcendentally, coupling it with the powerful secret of the *vitalization of things,* which is something above magnetism, because it couples magnetic fluidification with a soul that is intelligent on account of its power.

The word *vitalization* is inappropriate, but there is no other way of indicating the powerful magical means of coupling inanimate things not only with force but also with an intelligence that is living and keeps away contingent events.

Baron du Potet's experiment of the river in a room can be an example.

Let a strong magnetizer take a piece of charcoal and draw on the floor, with strong magnetic intention, two parallel lines, like this:

A ————————————
              River
B ————————————

and it must be understood that the two lines represent the two banks of a river.

Then we put a medium to sleep and we tell him, "Walk ahead."

The somnambulist walks. When he reaches line *A* he will stop. You say, "Walk on."

"I can't," he answers.

"Why not?"

"Because there is a river."

If you induce sleep in a second and a third subject, the result is the same. Let's suppose now that a magnetizer with a very strong fluidic projection draws the same two lines in the middle of a room without putting any medium to sleep; any sensitive person who comes into contact with those two lines will feel anxiety about something like the danger of turbulent waters.

Those who are very sensitive will stop and will perceive the thought of the person who drew the lines (telepathic correspondence).

From this, magnetizers draw the conclusion: *this is the secret of tal-ismans, signs, and operations of magic.*

But this is not a secret of magic, it is simply a magnetic operation, because if a magician draws the two lines with the intention of prevent-ing a specific man from crossing them, he succeeds without any other person having the slightest idea of the feeling that is meant for that specific man.

The magician takes not charcoal but any object that leaves no trace and draws a line *CD:*

C ——————————— D

He establishes that this will be an insurmountable obstacle for a Mr. Smith who must come. Now, that line is an obstacle only for Mr. Smith. Is this a question of magnetism, fluid, or intelligence'?

Let's go further on.

This Mr. Smith who must not go beyond the obstacle intuitively receives the warning that he must not go that way, even before he draws near. Perhaps in him there is something like a reasoned wish, the thought that it's better not to go that way; a hand keeps him back while a *spirit* speaks to him, giving him an excuse not to approach the area.

In this case magnetism is coupled with something, which is the secret of operators in magic and has nothing to do with known and recognized forces. The word *vitalizing* is imperfect because vitalization can be magnetic but not intelligent; that is, it is not capable of insight and judgment.

First of all, one must possess *will*, because a magician tries to end his career as he begins it, which is doing away with all means, and using only his wand as his scepter; because the scepter of modern-day kings is only the corruption of the magic wand of the Magi of the ancient priestly theocracy.

No doubt people nowadays would prefer the scepter of a live king to the wand of a magician they can't see: but the difference is that the wand of the invisible magicians calls the tune for earthly kings with their scepters, symbolic rods that are atrophied when those who hold them do not infuse them with the intelligence of Solomon.

Human society values highly an illustrious name, a noble family and their ancestors; without names, any vanity would be dead, and the pride of those who want to dominate their fellows, either through fame or the privilege of their origin or the prestige of academic honors, would be mortally wounded.

All those who wrote for and spoke to the masses in the name of science or absolute ideas were content to be humble soldiers, apostles, and not authors of the ideas they spread.

Who is the author of the Bible? Moses perhaps? Perhaps the builders of the second Temple?

Who is the author of Christianity? Jesus of Nazareth perhaps?

Who is the author of Plato's *Dialogues*? Plato perhaps?

Who is the author of the *Iliad* and the *Odyssey*? Homer perhaps?

Who is the author of *Le Roman de la Rose*?

Who is the author of the truth contained in *The Divine Comedy*?

Those who see and know are the artists of manifestations. The author of truth is Absolute Wisdom, that is Eternal Truth, whose profane, individual name is God.

In history, the authors of great renewals, of redemptions, of humanitarian revolutions are only names of ideas, the personification of absolute truth in relation to society and the times.

The mob believes that men are the authors of political changes in Greece, North America, England, Italy, but sound philosophy recognizes in each man a spirit of justice sent by the world of causes with the mission to accomplish divine will on earth.

The idea of freedom of the people, as well as the concept of human rights, and of the emancipation of women from servitude to male masters, the abolition of slavery, have no authors.

The apostles of those ideas are not, and will not be, their authors; they are, and will be, good or bad interpreters of universal laws.

The collective spirit always speaks through them, and God

incarnates and blesses it when it is a spirit of truth and justice, and no word is pronounced against it *up above* except when the spirit, incarnated for a mission, prevaricates and betrays it. This was the case with Napoleon, not to speak of more recent or contemporary men whose history everyone can learn to judge.

Part Three

THE
MYSTERIES
OF
THAUMATURGY

My dear Disciple,

Having discussed as clearly as possible the general principles of the two branches of *magic,* we must now face the scientific problem of *miracles* and *wonders* in the natural order of unchangeable laws.

Those who have not studied and practiced what I explained in the first part on natural and divine magic will find some sections of this part not very clear, because the philosophical speculation is related to general principles.

I warn you, as a student of the occult properties of the nature of things and of the human *spirit,* that in this second part I will begin to touch upon some terrible subjects, which, by divine law, cannot be communicated in full to uncultivated men without morals. This is why all ancient priestly sciences have always kept them veiled from the masses; and the Roman Catholic Church, which originates precisely from those religions and cults, has *re-veiled* them so thoroughly (that is, has little by little concealed so much of the truth in its rituals) that at the time of writing for vulgar Europe (the milk cow whose Italic calf would be marked, from the dark times of the people of Aeneas, as Christ the civilizer), the Catholic papacy has lost the keys to miracles and has become a prisoner of the vulgar society of the law of the masses, just as the human soul is a prisoner of the bestial body in those men who lose the light of the mind and identify all satisfaction with gross bodily senses.

Therefore, I am sowing the seed in the receptive and nourishing earth so that in the twentieth century the young philosopher of natural occult forces may patiently wait for the magician pope to again occupy the throne of Saint Peter, the fisher of souls, and so that the plant of occult knowledge finds the one who will perpetuate the truth, and not an abuser who violates human nature at his fellows' expense, because man must never use the science of the magicians to do evil. Christ on the Cross said: "Forgive them, O Lord, for they know not what they do." But would Christ have begged for forgiveness if his persecutors had known what they were doing? Therefore, it is not a crime to violate the laws of the divine world unknowingly, but it is an unforgivable sacrilege to violate them knowingly.

This is one of the basic reasons for the hierarchy of occult initiatory societies, a hierarchy criticized so much by advocates of the average level of intelligences, which contributes to the whole procession of errors and misery in the world, and which, in turn, leads to the divine punishment of human society.

My dear reader, at the beginning of the first book I told you that the dabbler has no right to superhuman knowledge. Now it is time for you to form an exact idea of the mission of *superior men within humanity* and to see clearly the sin of modern positivist and materialist zoological philosophy and the sin of priestly ignorance as the two most terrible scourges of the present day, physically illuminated by electric light and morally unenlightened by the egotistic doctrine of sensualist satisfaction.

On a day of popular merrymaking, of public feasting, look out of your window at the human wave that floods the streets. Close your eyes for a moment and imagine that a hundred years have gone by. Reopen your eyes and, facing the deserted streets, think that the thousands of people swarming a moment earlier in those same streets are dead and returned to dust.

If you do this while you are alive, you will have learned that the life of man, like the life of the masses in the heat of the physical senses, is the deceitful voluptuousness of the void. Men and generations pass by like lightning, and what we call a century disappears like soap bubbles or become piles of bones rotting in cemeteries.

If you do this, and reflect closely, you may become a saint or a sinner. You will become a sinner if you think that, as the body and the senses are vain, so is *morality;* you will become a saint if you think that the *spirit of the earth* feeds on the daily slaughter of so many different human bodies, over which floats *the genius of races* and the soul of the purified man, who has become, as Dante says, Intelligence separated from matter, whose home is beyond the commonplace and false logic of the senses.

But every soap bubble has a soul; the child who blows through a straw into soapy water would not make bubbles if he did not *blow out.* Therefore, each bubble contains a breath, or a spirit, a soul, a thought, an ideal.

If the soap bubble bursts, has its breath, its spirit, its soul vanished and died? Alternatively, while the body bears its heavy burden back to the earth, waiting to be broken down, might not the spirit fuse itself with the universal breath and return to the chaos of the *spirit of the world?* Or else might it not still be a breath, a thought in the process of evolution?

This is the problem of the Sphinx, of veiled Isis, of the Cross, of the five-pointed *Star,* of the ineffable Word expressing the name of Jehovah. This is the incommunicable secret of the ancient schools of magic, capable of all miracles and wonders.

But the secret corresponding to this *absolute truth* is not a vain point of discussion for academics: magic is a useless thing if it remains theoretical, but if it is realized in practice, it becomes the most powerful lever in the four streams of the Edenic cross:

1. Religion, which governs the soul of the masses
2. Human society (the State)
3. Common knowledge
4. Art

Magic, or *absolute science,* conflicts with religion when the priests of the latter have lost the key; with human society, when the latter walks in the shadows, illuminating thought with the senses; with profane science, when the finitude of imperfect reason wants to know and judge the *infinitude* of the invisible; with art, when this eternal manifestation of the greatest ideal gets mired in the mud of a *mannerism* beyond the two extremes of plastic reality and poetic creation.

The godless, the titans of profane science, would build a new Tower of Babel, and would try to climb the heavens with matter. The eternal satanic struggle of the spirit against God becomes eternal in this forced march of the philosophy of the senses against the absolute—the *simple and great soul* that governs the spirit and the matter of the created worlds.

So, human societies, at the mercy of materialist reason, fall into the abyss of matter; so the Providence of the divine world is denied; so it is believed, written, taught, preached, and evangelized that Spirit is matter and that human thought is the only providential path for the masses to follow toward the infinite of the history of social and earthly suffering.

So many lies!

And yet the history, which should instruct us, is there; not the anecdotal and wretched history of society in evolution, but the monuments of races and nations witnessing, in myriad soapy bubbles, the presence of the *chosen souls* of the incarnations of spirits, evolved or sent here to fulfill the heroic mission of fighting the serpent of error and cutting off its head.

But the fight is there, between the materialized souls of the masses and the prolific spirit of Jehovah; the rebellious angels are embodied in the philosophy of the state, in the doctrinal egotism of states, in the materialistic investigation of the spirit of things, in the mental unrest determining revolutions without science, while the messengers from the beyond in times of crisis and infirmity in the masses, put things right and go off again.

Look for their names in the history of religions, of philosophy, of science, of personal liberty, and you will always perceive the divine light shadowed by the reason of human pride.

Therefore, to approach, through Magic and the study of its theory and practice, the shores of the vast Ocean of the Real Truth means either to be changed into an angel, or to be changed into a devil, or to be killed by one's own reason and daring, without even justifying oneself before human society and its history.

•◆•

So the *mysteries of the prime causes,* O disciple, begin to lead you by the hand through the hell of human knowledge, in the search for the reason behind miracles and wonders; but your search, your tiring mission, will be a totally wasted effort if you do not *practice.* Practice alone gives, in our science, the right to arrive; but the key to all practice depends on the sanctity of the disciple: without sanctity or the subsequent purification of your spirit, you will never accomplish divine work, and if you manage to do something without sanctity, you will be doing the devil's work.

To become a saint?

Here is a paradox for the reader who is well informed about scientific studies and modern methods, but we must understand sanctity not as the masses understand devotion and bigotry; *the saint is he who identifies his human reason with the fatal reason of things and of spirits. The saint is an altruist who considers himself as a traveler in a hotel, during a stop on his journey toward the infinite, final evolution of all created things. The saint is he who has the wisdom not to delude himself about visible reasons and who makes himself worthy of the science of God.*

So you will find your sanctification only in *love for your fellow,* and so you become a lesser Jesus of Nazareth and will sacrifice yourself voluntarily, loving your neighbors, extending your hand to your brother to redeem him and lead him to spiritual enlightenment, and in your hands Magic will reproduce ancient legendary wonders, your rod will blossom, and you will sow goodness all around you; and while a part of mankind thinks and illuminates the other part with electric light, you will be a soldier of this other part, and you will be a beacon to the souls on this earthly journey . . . to stop repeating it or to repeat it at will.

•◆•

Philosophy is studied, ideas are discussed, symbols are explained, but in order to learn the magical art after you have learned the philosophy of magic, you must possess three things:

1. *Will* without desire
2. The *strength* to act without ceasing
3. The *practice* of not making mistakes

He who *desires* is unable to *will*. Desire is an appetite of illusion, which paralyzes will, whose mechanism becomes most perfect in the absence of any desire. The man who *desires* a woman becomes her slave; if, on the contrary, he wills her, he makes her his slave. The man who *desires* money is a miserable beggar of fortune; but he who wills it, dominates it. The magician who desires is not a magician and does not work miracles. But nobody can exactly tell where *desire* ends and *will* begins; only *your* philosophy can explain it to you.

The second necessary thing is *strength*. Do you know why a seed planted in sea sand bears no fruit, but when sown in a vegetable garden bears fruit? Because the sea sand is rich in salt and is not productive, and the earth of the vegetable garden has the *strength to give life* without ceasing. That is why the magician must possess the strength to transform himself into the individual forces of nature to produce, like nature, all its miracles and wonders; he must have the strength to nourish the seed like the earth of the garden, or to destroy it like the salt of the sea sand. The strength to continue without ceasing is like this in the immutable constancy of nature, and it is the same in those who want to work miracles.

The third quality is *practice*. The inexperienced child who picks roses pricks his fingers and sees them bleed, but the gardener can pick many of them without pricking his hands. In the magical art, he who knows how to produce and does not produce is like the sword maker who makes the weapon for war and does not go to war.

The magician becomes an *artist* after being a philosopher, through the development of his faculties, that is, by the virtue of his *spirit*. This magician's spirit, placed in and fed by the human body, has two great prerogatives that disembodied spirits do not have: *the power to transform into force, and the freedom to materialize.*

As soon as the magician begins to work by himself, his plastic soul becomes the flame of life that descends and goes up, as the ancient Hermeticists used to say. It means that his spirit lives on the earth and in space, and only when the spirit of man living in the flesh has acquired the power to go up, that is, to come up to the surface of the astral current, is he capable of subjugating all the creatures of the current or ocean that forms the aura of the earth.

When I annotated a book* of the Esoteric Library, I explained the interpretation of the icthys, or fish, the symbol of the Christ of the earlier Christians; but the symbol of the fish belongs to the Essenes, a sect from which Jesus of Nazareth came, which had taken figurative symbolism from the writings of Egyptian priests; whereas the pure Hebraic rites do without symbols and make use of the literal signs of the Kabbalah, which correspond to ideas, things, and numbers, just as the Pythagorean system expresses absolute ideas by whole numbers and relative ideas by combinations of numbers in multiples and submultiples.

The Hebraic thaumaturgic figures consist of lines, straight and curved, geometric in appearance; the Egyptian ones are figurative, anthropomorphic; and the Pythagorean ones are numerals.

The Christ—that is, the soul of man that goes up to the heavens or down to the depths at will—was symbolized as a fish that, using its fins and swimming bladders, comes up to the surface of the water or, at will, goes down to the deepest caverns of the ocean.

Like the fish in the water, so the soul of man in the astral light. Only when the soul of man has acquired the power of going up and down like the fish can it operate in harmony with the intellectual ultra-astral powers; before attaining this state, the common man is symbolized by the turtle and the snail, which represent the astral body in the heavy container of fleshy matter.

That is why *natural magic,* the easier of the two types, makes use only of forces that belong to the embodied human spirit and to the

*[*Cristo, la Magia e il Diavolo* (Christ, Magic, and the Devil), by Éliphas Lévi, with descriptive notes by Dr. Giuliano Kremmerz (Detken and Rochell, 1898). —*Ed.*]

inferior *animals of the astral zone,* and that is why it is susceptible to good and evil, to useful and deadly works, and makes use of materialized fluids and horrible animals of the astral.

• ◆ •

As I said in the opening pages, my treatise on natural and divine magic must be a clear explanation not of what others have said but of what really is. For this reason, I pray my readers who want to be practical form a precise idea for themselves of what we are.

Take a very large crystal vase, fill it with water, and put freshwater fish, eels, and water beetles into it. Looking at the water and the fish through the glass you, the human being, are—compared with the animals in the liquid—what an intelligence of a superior order (*purified spirit* or *archangel*) is, compared with we who are immersed in the astral current, while the three types of aquatic animal in the liquid (beetles, eels, and fish) represent three different stages in the development of the human spirit.

I say *human spirit* because, in man, spirit is not separate from matter, and therefore we must emphasize that the spirit in man carries with it that amount of purified matter (*diaphanous, astral body, peri-spirit*) that is inherent to its development. The heavier the container, the more ponderous the matter that envelops it, the less sensitive the intelligent spirit is.

Now pass from looking at the crystal vase of fish to observing life in the ocean. Form your own notion, even an approximate one, of all that is in the ocean, from phosphorescent protozoa to swordlike seaweeds, from protoplastic mollusks to prawns, from goldfish to dolphins, from sharks to whales, and, by analogy, you will have pictured the animal life in the astral ocean, which, starting from the life of stones, passes through plant life to the instinctive intelligence of microbes, and from there scales the animal ladder to man.

Darwin formulated the most farsighted theory of linked relationship in animal evolution, and the same distinction applies to the intellect. From the dog to the elephant, from the monkey to man, there is a gradual progression in intellectual terms, reaching its peak in *Homo sapiens;* but in this human species there always exists a hierarchical link that intellectually binds men to all the races. There are some men who are barely more intelligent than the most intelligent dog, as there are others who border on pure evolved spirits, no longer alive to human life.

Those who want to understand the language of the gods must penetrate the language of primitive syntheses, passing beyond the abyss of human languages.

The sacred Kabbalah, the secret philosophy of the absolute, has the power of making the synthetic language of divine ideas eternal. Before the scientific processes of common knowledge it is the torch that recalls civilizations sealed with the priestly knowledge of things.

The Kabbalah is the philosophy of absolute laws and of the immutable elements of physical, intelligent, and mental nature, of nature in its concrete expression.

The numerical Kabbalah, or occult Pythagorean tradition, owing to the substitution of *numbers* for *words,* is even more difficult to grasp without the help of a *fluent master.*

The Arabs had and have angels with two or more eyes. The bodily eyes represent their humanization, while the extra eyes refer to their divinity. So, with our human eyes we can see the physical sun, and with the mental eyes, the sun of the archetypal world. I say it clearly: the master starts talking only when the concave and convex—as the old rabbis said—of the celestial world shine with incandescence to the vision of the mental eye.

To study the Kabbalah without the will to understand the syntheses is a waste of time.

Moses received the fifty doors of divine intelligence as a gift from Jehovah, the God whose name consists of *four symbolic letters,* and Moses handed them down to us. In order to understand well how this legacy has feathered our nest, we must remember that the word *Moses* has different meanings, some of which are occult, incommunicable, and others of which are manifest; one of the most widely known is that

Moses means "attracted to God" or "saved from the waters." From what waters? Those of the Nile? Or might not the Nile and its waters rather be the astral river, which floods the profane and fleshly Egypt of the Pharaohs, the kings of matter?

The mental eye must go further and deeper than the human eye when scrutinizing books and sacred truths.

The synthetic, ideological, Kabbalistic language is imprecise in that it may lend itself to interpretations, which at times may be false and profane, at times divine. A deep knowledge of the Kabbalah clarifies the perception of the concrete order of immutable nature. The intellectual light allows us a deep perception of all the manifestations imperceptible to the profane eye.

Nature, matter, spirit, the visible, and the invisible are but one. The unity is God. All fatal events are God's will. Life, death, pain, joy are forms and moments of the universal psychic life. Jehovah is the *ego sum qui sum* [I am that I am], and all truths are in him, the *semoth* of the Kabbalists (mystical science) and *sophisath* (numerical science): in him and for him all the manifestations of living and intelligent nature.

The prophecy is only in this: high magic is in the interpretation of the whole of nature as the language of the Only and Immutable Almighty. Clairvoyance is the synthesis of the impression of universal nature.

So-called superstitions are but the language of the invisible but inferior life. Dreams represent a life and a great truth only for those who can analogically read their real and deep significance.

A word is the materialization of an idea. It is the act generated by the *idea*. The men who study philology in ordinary schools are not competent in the magnetic and magic technique of the word. Pythagorean silence was deemed appropriate for canceling the impurities attached to the phonic or graphic signs of *human thought* or of the absolute world of *everlasting truths*. Soul, life, and thought are words, sounds, and signs; they are effects and works; they are calculations and monuments; they are sensations and they are . . . nothingness.

Sensations may and may not be effective in determining the truth of what exists. The two factors should be memory and will; consciousness is but the persistent feeling resulting from the whole working of the three factors:

sensibility
persistent memory (irrefutable evidence, consciousness)
will

Sensibility is misleading, memory may be equally misleading, will may be dominated by a will of greater dynamism. Consequently, the evidence of *truth* must come from a sense that is subtler, deeper, higher than simple animal or sensory consciousness.

Consciousness is a *sensation* to the extent that it is the result of complex and separate actions of things upon the human body: the animal nature of man, of man balanced according to zoosophical theory, cannot have consciousness beyond the feeling of memories and of completed actions that took place.

But the psychically advanced man has a *second consciousness,* which is not the result of physical actions, and which contains a certain inexpressible, luminous sense, which detaches and separates the two arrows resulting from the equation of the free individualized power of the ether of Hippocrates and of the external current.

I will clarify with an example. Being thirsty, take a bottle of good wine. Drink it. As the wine is introduced to the stomach, you become increasingly drunk. Then you are *conscious* of the action of the wine on your brain.

Until you are completely drunk, you have the exact awareness of lightheadedness influencing your actions. This deep feeling, which puts you above the physical effects of the action of the wine, was presented by some philosophical sects as the dynamic, intelligent duplicate of soul consciousness.

Here it is in graphic form:

Wine—its action
Lightheadedness
Drunkenness
Delirium
} *animal consciousness*   material soul

The intellectual
sense judging the
abnormal state
} *intellective consciousness*   intelligent soul

But that is not enough: over and above this supersensitive consciousness there is the judging principle, the *inner self,* the free and rational soul principle, judging both kinds of consciousness.

•◆•

To those who asked me one day why occultists did not express their ideas clearly, that the reason why must be sought in the very imperfect nature of the disciples, in whom the involutional act represented by original sin, of which Catholic baptism is meant to purify, leads all creatures to the complete and concrete materialization of the most sublime ideas and the highest conceptions, which are neither *human* nor *humanizable;* otherwise they would be finite and would belong to hell or the netherworld of error.

The Kabbalah of the rabbis is the Immaculate Conception outside any blemish of human prevarication. Words are expressions and misrepresentations of conceived ideas. To speak means to make material. To speak is to dissolve. To listen to speech is to deviate if one does not go beyond the words spoken and does not grasp the ideas behind them. The great mystery lies in the silence of the senses to allow the evolution or purification of the embodied spirit.

Remember, my disciple, that human doctrines, I mean those which do not have their foundation in the purification of the human spirit and its evolution toward the recovery of its earliest freedom, were called *diabolic, satanic, infernal,* just because they tried to set up an altar in opposition to the evolution of the spirit. The attempt to conquer the heavens, violating them by making sublime ideas concrete, is *titanic;* but the titans are the spirits most deeply embedded in the mud, who tend to mix any abstract and pure idea with the mud, thus making the mud sublime.

The dogma of the omnipotence of the God-Being (Tetragrammaton) contains the union of two active elements acting upon the same passive element. But if the universe or macrocosm contains this absolute power, the microcosm or man (God-Man) contains, by analogy, the same elements.*

The modern world cannot explain why learned men for so many centuries have been very interested in the definitions of the fundamental ideas of religion; it is because this contemporary world of ours cannot grasp the *positiveness* of wise theological dissertations and the meaning of the abstract formulae on which the seemingly verbose discussions were based. The silliest and most abstruse provisions in the eyes of the moderns, who do not try to penetrate the fundamentals of religious motivations, all concealed a strong tendency toward realization; from the Manes to the Catholic heresies of recent centuries, the heresiarchs— but those who really deserved the name—all had in the bottom of their brains a special idea for the manifestation and disintegration of truth. The first centuries of Christian Rome, when nascent Christianity found itself in doctrinal conflict with all the philosophical systems of pagan Latinity, saw the fervent struggle between the philosophical systems, because, at that time, even the revealed doctrine of the neo-Christians was conceived as a system of philosophical doctrines. The different ways of conceiving and of defining the *Creative Unity* and its manifestations gave birth to three main streams of applied wisdom:

1. The aim of life and how to achieve it
2. Morality and social trends
3. Reason, history, and political realization

*Yod, Heh, Vau, Heh: Jehovah

From the concrete ideal of the human Mind, acting as a reflector of universal power, a different moral tendency is projected on social surroundings, and when modern philosophers come and enlarge upon the eighteenth-century idea of the nonexistence of *absolute morality*, they show that the work of great religions from Buddhism to Christianity has passed before their eyes as a fleeting image because they have not understood that the social factor, which prepares the way for the great revolutions and the great historical ideas, is the religious ideal, which gives birth to the morality and well-being of the people.*

Please notice that now I am speaking to those readers who are deeply interested in social sciences, showing them, without any bigotry and above all religions, a new standpoint from which to look at and understand the beneficial influence of all religious activity for all modern civilized peoples, and I think I would be straying from the path if I tried to widen the discussion of the subject. I here must only remind the reader that magic, the perfect science, must not be understood only as the manifestation of the occult powers of a man on other men or things, but of the human mind as the manifestation of divine harmony over the whole historical milieu in the course of long epochs.

The ordinary life of a man, much shorter than a century, does not prove anything in the practical reality of life. Jesus of Nazareth was only able, in his life, if the symbolism of his story is truthful, to be tormented. But out of his torments, from the cross on which he was nailed, through the *consummatum est* [It is completed],† he worked

---

*Divine science can be entrusted only to pure men, that is, men who have no personal interest and are consequently free from needs and ambitions. To follow the road of the secret science of the magicians through a disinterestedness that is only apparent is sorcerer's work. Egotism is the benchmark. Egotism is the touchstone of all initiates. The theocratic governments of ancient times were not based on religious industry, as the young are ordinarily led to believe, but they marked the guidance of peoples by enlightened men acting *out of disinterestedness*.

†[Christ's final words on the cross in the Latin Vulgate translation of the New Testament, John 19:30. —*Ed.*]

the greatest act of social magic: he prepared the way for new times; he set in motion the idea of equilibrium, which twenty centuries later is not yet completely realized and alive. But if the master had lived in his human form for twenty centuries, and if the human memory were strong enough to embrace in one wonderful picture all the work done, we could exclaim, as Napoleon did at the Pyramids, that forty centuries will look with admiration upon the glorious work of the most glorious of the ideal masters. The human magic of a sectarian and of a Hebrew sect is created through religion and philosophy, wisdom, progress, light, and social perfection. Take the head of a man, break it open, describe the organs it contains. If it is in the bleeding brain that you look for the man, if it is in its weight that you want to find the idea, then you are compelled to draw two great consequences: the absolute materiality of life, and the sensualist orgy as the only social aim. One draws the obvious moral that the great errors of satanic rites in those who, even in simply studying theology, overturn it for a determined purpose and for the achievement of immediate success. In magic only the pure or impure conception defines the application and the tendency of the rites, which may be great, on account of their ideality or their foulness. The same is true for religion and politics.

•◆•

I said that to the head of man or upper vertex of the magical pentacle—which Éliphas Lévi rightly advises us never to trace because it is never traced with impunity—correspond the signs of magisterial or divine microcosmic omnipotence, ☉ + ☽, but if we want to philosophize on this principle of the binary residing in the human mind or embodied spirit, we must place the two signs differently:

$$+ \; ☽$$
$$☉$$
$$- \; ☾$$

The upper lunar crescent waxing *positive* in ideality, and the lower waning and *passive.*

In the positive you have the key of Isis or Immaculate Conception.

In the passive, you have the formula of the corruption of purity or Persephone.

The ⊙ intelligence is between the two factors. Human free will lies exactly in this choice, but in working magic, once the choice has been made, one must face the consequences.

God is One. In Psalm 138 the Latin Vulgate line 8 is:

> *Si adscendero in coelum, tu illic es;*
> *Si descendero ad infernum ades.*
> [If I ascend into heaven, you will be there;
> If I descend into hell, you will be there.]

That "tu" refers to *Dominus qui intelligit cogitationes et cognoscit sensions* [He who understands thoughts and experiences sensations]: therefore, the *dominus* is above and below.*

Here I beg my readers not to put his foot in it and to reflect well on what I am saying, because those who can grasp the real meaning of my words will achieve the result of coming face to face with the truth, as Jacob fought in close combat with the mystic angel, and was lamed in one leg.

Since the truth, which so many sacred symbols and so many evocative formulae veil, which so many sublime or nefarious acts symbolize or search for, is not the *word* that manifests the secret name of God, but the attempt to hand it down without pronouncing it, that is, without violating it, to posterity, so that those who merit it may

---

*This unity God cannot be clearly understood by the public who study the secret Kabbalah without blasphemy: God is the Devil. But to formulate the law in this way is absurd, because it would be a negation of the binary. Ask a professor of theology if God in the home of the Devil is or is not God. Those who do not understand the question should not reflect too much on these words, or they might stay in "infernum" without finding God there.

learn it and hear it repeated in their ears as the greatest conquest of absolute wisdom.*

The reverberations of this truth are prismatic. There is a wave of seven colors of truth, which men grasp and admire, according to greater or lesser perfection of their spirits. The whole luminous spectrum is the truth of the great masters; only one of the colors is the more-or-less miraculous power of the aspirants to the final adeptship.

The moment of final conquest, when the *master* is formed, is a moment of rebirth. From the caterpillar bursts forth the mystical butterfly of Dante Alighieri and then, prostrated before the blinding truth, one looks on the ocean of human impurities as from a flying balloon, on the blackness of the tarry bog of the ancient visionaries.

The kingdom of beatitude of Buddha and the Assumption of Mary in Catholic doctrine are identical as states of perfectibility desired by initiates. To penetrate the limbo of higher purity + ☽ is the way to get there; to fall into the − ☾ is the magic of involutional forms. The clairvoyance in all fields and the high perfection of the highest embodied priests belong to the former; all the illusions of the astral zone, all the imperfections and the volubility of the current of the involutional souls belong to the latter. Behind this double aspect of the efforts of the initiates to reach the state of conquest, the terrible secret of the life and death of human souls† is hidden.

Io parlo per ver dire,‡ and do not think that the author of the *Divine Comedy* was trying his hand at philosophy and history without inspira-

---

*To this end, the first part must be read and reread. The secret of the incommunicable word can be given by a master who knows it, or stolen from him by one who is close to him and avoids being dismissed when the master perceives the danger of his devotion. We must not forget that the disciple is the true sponge of the master only when the disciple succeeds, and that, vice versa, he is absorbed by the master when he becomes an insignificant number in his chain. Arnon used to say to his disciple: "In order to succeed in magic it is not enough to find a master. It is necessary not to lose him and not to let him go."

†The reader should not take this as a misprint. I do say: the *life and death of human souls.*

‡[I speak to tell the truth. —*Trans.*]

tion and a clear vision of the truth. The man who is beyond sensism is faced with the choice: Christ or Satan. In common doctrines, Christ represents the world of the perfection of souls, whereas Satan represents all that is of matter and the senses.

⊙   *in coelum illic es*   (PSALM 138)
                  in infernum ades

Do not understand, if you have any respect for intellect, as the false gnostics of the early centuries did, *that above and below are one* and that all is *duality;* do not understand that the psalmist confused omnipotence with the transformation of the divine personage into the king of Hell in the infernal spheres, but reflect upon the fact that Pythagoras called man both *unity* and *multiplicity,* and the origin, or God, he called one.

In Catholic symbolism the Virgin Mary represents the Immaculate Conception above the active zone of pagan intellectuality (Minerva) and, with the waning moon of which I spoke above under her feet, she is free from any terrestrial effluvium: passively religious men aspire to this state of purification. The litanies of the Madonna must be read and studied in every appellation, from which one can infer the scale of all the qualities attributed to purity.

This symbolism of the Immaculate Conception goes back many centuries before Christ. The veiled Isis of Egypt and the female or lunar divinities of the Assyrian and Babylonian monarchies are proof of this. It is the highest cult from the philosophical and magical point of view. But this cult lends itself to decay in sacrilegious ceremonies as soon as the stainless purity of this sublime ideal of mental exaltation is stained with quite material acts of coercion and imprecations. In this case, not infrequently, the purest ideality becomes confused with spiritual decadence of the effigies magnetized and enchanted to produce certain effects: so each image corresponds to a title and each title corresponds to the desire for a favor or a satisfaction of personal needs.

I have gone on at some length about the symbolism of Mary and the Christian Conception to make those who call themselves strong *spirits* understand well that in supreme theosophy *Mary* and the *Conception* are but states of mental light, the same as the mystical rose of the Rosicrucians. The truth, which places at its feet all the mutability influencing the terrestrial world (the moon), is surrounded by twelve stars: they are the astral appearances, which never change, and yet which shine with the same light and the same intensity around the smiling head of Wisdom.

But the cult of statues and images and the visions such as those of Lourdes and of the other Madonnas is inferior to the pure and highest symbolism of the *Mater Dei*. The many who had visions of the Madonna do not rise above the astral visions where the spirit of *humanity* speaks through symbols to the intelligence of the visionary. On the other hand, not all can apprehend the Purest among the Virgins in the ideal field, and the images, statues, paintings are real evocations of the ideal. Let every sufferer turn to her and he will receive comfort; the sick man will be blessed and healed. If he who prays is not capable of raising himself to the highest of the purest heights, let him evoke and invoke his astral image (*in-magus*), and even the shadow of that light is a light that consoles. Here is the month of flowers . . . the mystical rose is on the cross of universal equilibrium in the name of which the master sends a greeting to the brothers scattered in the universe and waiting for the New Sun.

In sorcerers' rites Astarte, like Persephone in the Orphic rites, instead of keeping the moon at her feet, lets the horns of the moon emerge from her hair. The moon with the horns upward stands on her head. A sinuous body like that of a serpent, monstrous in her lust, enchanting in her form, is the Parthenopean Siren of the ancient seafarers. The Siren enticingly enchants those who travel in search of the truth. How will you conquer her, if your heart trembles and your flesh creeps at her voluptuous song? Ulysses says, "Stop your ears with wax"; but Ulysses's story is famous, and I do not have to repeat it or comment on it here. The master who takes his disciple on board on the voyage to the conquest of truth must test him and throws him onto the shore where the Siren lies in wait for lovers and victims. He gives in to her: too bad for him! He saves himself: good for him!

To sum up:

Every kind of thaumaturgy has its foundation in Light. *Light* par excellence is either God or the Devil: if my reader has clearly understood the line from Psalm 138 quoted above, before feeling puffed up with wisdom based on arguments, he must first learn to ask *a child with the eyes of an old man* if he should turn for light to the lamplighter on high or to the one from the unknown hell of the living. But, and above all, he must not start from the preconceived ideas, which the pretentions and profane education of so many centuries have been forcing into the psyche of contemporary races. The *fiat lux* is known in theory; algebraically everybody thinks that an Almighty Spirit may have created Light, but if you reflect on the first problems of occult philosophy, which I had the honor of explaining to my disciple at the beginning of the first part of *Il Mondo Secreto,* the frightful dilemma of discovering the God living within yourself is not an unorthodox task, since all Christian churches teach the faithful that man is made in the image of God. If, before the creation, God had an active creative power, then after the creation, that is, once he is embodied and individualized in man, he must preserve the capability of his essential creative potential.

My reader, open wide the ears of your spirit and the eyes of your mind, because if you fail to grasp the aphoristic meaning of this first arcanum that I am laying out before you, you will speculate in vain on the virtue of communicating the understanding of the accomplished miracle to yourself.

The sectarians of the first Christian centuries said that the double God, emanator of true and living light, was Light and Serpent. The Ophites believed in the Serpent, as San Alfonso Maria de' Liguori teaches, and those who came after them laughed only at those wise men and their symbology among all the dangerous sectarians and revolutionaries of the incubation period of primitive Christianity. Theodoret in his long diatribes against the Pythagoreans, by means of popular eloquence, made certain suggestions that the Gentiles and those who lived before the introduction of Essenism to Europe never meant to symbolize occult mysteries of secret spiritual nature in divinized persons. The ancient world, as regards matters of spiritual sciences, was far more advanced than eighteenth-century controversies or the polemical discussions of the end of this century, and the only point, which historically divides the periods, is the vulgarization of the number, that is to say the widening of the first and limited circle of wisdom considered as high priestly manifestation. Magic must absorb all the exteriority of Eternal Religion of which Buddhism, Brahmanism, Egypto-Chaldeanism, Paganism, and Christianity are only glimpses of the truth in the vastness of time. *Magic is the science.*

The times are the *morality:* morality, the key to the science of religious forms, lies in customs. *Mores sunt tempora* [the morals are the times]; the famous *tempora* or *mores* is a one-way expression—the spiritual degree (with its great influence upon human society) dictates the upward progress of human society.

The outer face of the gods is popular or profane, that is, it is the imitation or the example of past ages. But did the actions of profane people accord with the secret face of these gods? Does Janus, the god with two faces, teach nothing to the would-be philosophers of ancient mythologies?

I advise the study of mythology in its essence, as you may find in it the initiation of the powers of our organism; it is the search for a rare science, the possibility of unveiling an arcanum of integration.

The initiate into the magic of the priesthood must not consider the simple outer image of divinities; he must penetrate their occult aspects, because if you do not know the secret face of God, you are deluded in thinking yourself a philosopher learned in orthodox and hieratical sciences.

To ask the *Master* for a book in which miracles are taught in the same way as card games is a cowardly lie of the vulgar spirit. You must ask for and obtain light before the *Master* speaks, otherwise his words are like pearls cast before swine.

If you want to take away the last veil between you and occult truth, you may evoke either of these two forms: the objective (the reflection or specter) or the subjective (the Fire or Matrix).

The first of these ways is easier and longer.

Religious orders confirm this. A slow and meditative reading of the *Imitation* by Thomas à Kempis or the methodical regimen of a religious order, perhaps from the Far East, prepares you for the evocation of the living Christ.

The active magical orders prepare you for the second way.

Creative Fire, outside of all created things, of all personalities and personifications, represents the dilemma of the victory or annihilation of the active and enquiring spirit. The incredible bravery of the evocations of pyro-magic cannot be appreciated even as the invention of a novelist. But after your conquest, the last veil falls from your eyes and you understand the *Master.*

Here begins the thaumaturgic work of the adept.

Without first making a bold attempt to destroy yourself, atom by atom, in order to see the face of the one whose real face, it is written, no one ever saw, whose voice was heard only by the one saved from the waters, and whom Christ called Father, you must not try to perform miracles.

Those who want to start by performing miracles in order to then make up their minds, act like madmen in the science of secret truth, which is *magic.*

The first aspect of God's ray, kabbalistically known by the name of *Ariel,* is the thaumaturgic power or capacity to perform miracles, which miracles are not, as profane and ignorant men think, breaches of the laws of nature; neither are they, as pseudo-scientists of the normality of events would have us believe, due in great part to the ignorance of the believers.

Secret sciences maintain that miracles are real and evident acts of creation through the same creative laws by which Jehovah performed the great miracle of the creation of the universe.

The laws and conceptions of the miracle are the basis of the second sense of the Kabbalah, and the *Intelligence* of theosophy is represented by the quinary of which we have spoken.

Ariel is an angel, that is, he is the form of the force expressed by divine intelligence. Therefore, he is force and he is intelligence. He is instinctively strong and intelligent. He is *capable.*

In profane mysticism all that comes from material life of things, all that includes the double act of value and deliberative capacity is *Ariel,* who is the evocation or manifestation of Jehovah's face.

In the life of matter there is very slow motion; in the life of thought there is rapid rotary motion. We must distinguish and divide intellectuality from materialization.

Therefore, in the practice of magic, the names of divine entities must be understood and comprehended as having a threefold application:

1. *Intelligence* or projection of central divine will
2. *Spirit* or manifestation of tendency
3. *Genius* or *daimon* in their real manifestation

Each of these forms has a different phenomenal manifestation.

In the first, the phenomenon is mental; in the second, it is astral; in the third, it is material, that is, it belongs to the world visible to ordinary people.

Ariel in divine magic is the absolute intelligence of the divine creative force. Intelligence means comprehension, penetration, subtle intuition of the value of the power of creation. In its second phase of adaptation, it is a *spirit* or an *angel* acting on the astral current. In its third appearance, it is the act of materialized force; that is, the incarnation of intelligence.

Before we go further it is necessary for the disciple to understand this difference practically, otherwise he cannot exactly understand *magic,* the science of the most perfect. On the contrary, owing to the rapid and misleading effects of an imprecise interpretation that, to him thinking wrongly about magical things, offers certain things like *experimental spiritualism* and psychical studies that tend to form a body of abstract, incomplete, and misleading doctrines that will falsely appear to be very deep and more concrete because they start from sensation and physical objectivity with the ultimate result that they go back to . . . the source of sensation itself.

To study *Magic* and apply Theurgy does not mean to study the phenomena perceptible to the physical senses, but to study the occult laws and produce visible phenomena; and, like all sciences, Magic must be studied attentively first in its doctrinal aspect and then in its application; however, before learning anything that has to do with the science, one must understand the sense of the words that one uses.

The words *angel, demon,* and *spirit* do not have the same meaning from a scientific point of view as the public has given them, and a student of modern science well up in the research in operating theaters and bacteriological laboratories, basing himself on his scientific background, finds the three words contemptible, as they express laughable concepts. Perhaps I will be the last as well as the first to rehabilitate the ancient classical "logology" of occult science to create the link between ancient and modern forms of human knowledge aiming at the apotheosis of divine synthetic wisdom; but in the future *those who come after me will only represent my complete transformation into modernity, and the world will welcome as very modern discoveries things that belong to the ancient knowledge of the priesthood of the one science.* Now, it would seem extremely odd and strange for a professor of chemistry in a modern university to invoke in front of his disbelieving students, before trying an experiment, the angel of transformation of Mercury or the demon of mutation of the Moon. In spite of all this, the titanic castle of wise mankind will keep rising layer by layer and by superimposing theories, as well as by *insufflations* of so-called *scientific* ideas in order to graft, over many generations, the germ of novelty in the consciousness of true things of the visible world.

One day will come, and it is not very far away, when people will understand what *human life* is and then, whatever "socialists" and "humanists" of our time may say, the discoverers of this great truth, which is the secret of the tree of good and evil, will understand that their only means of salvation is to set themselves up as a scientific theocracy. The two discoveries of this dying century, X-rays and wireless communication, although wonderful, are insignificant as compared with the scientific solution of the problem of *human life*. The highest initiation gives this secret to the adepts, but how many ever get so far?

My present task is to gather the select few together. The seeds of this science will find in them the fruitful earth to make them masters for coming generations, that is, to sow in them the seed of eternal truth above all artifice of arrogant human science. I am speaking to them so that they may *understand* before *practicing,* so that they may not *practice* empirically like charlatans, to stumble while they think they are studying magic into the blind alley of popular spiritualism or mesmeric somnambulism, foundations for doctrines without beginning or end.

Magic cannot be practiced like a profession learned by human will: it is the practice of *active virtues*. It *cannot* and *does not* exist for those who practice it according to the blind and incoherent theory of well-known practices. Those who do Magic with this sad and imperfect habit of producing immediate phenomena practice the crudest kind of spiritualism, but those who want to produce magical effects without the *knowledge* of what they are doing sow in the sand, and dreadful catastrophes result from their madness. This madness does not only result in the death of the physical body, as they may think; it often results in the second death, that is, the complete annihilation of their psychical entity. This is the warning before which any imprudent work must stop.

In order to understand before practicing, one must fully realize all the theories, analogies, and words used in the *Great Art,* or *Ars Magna,* the explication of the highest divine science.

Everything in practical Magic is achieved through love; love is divine intelligence, that is, a state of understanding, it is the intuition of the divine embrace between finite matter and the infinite world.

Each evocation or invocation is an effort of understanding.

If this effort is directed toward inferior aims, that is, toward finite bodies having a determined evolutive life, it represents the involution of one's own being into nether life (hell, diabolism, witchcraft).

If, on the contrary, it tends toward God, that is, toward the supreme Infinite Almighty, it represents evolution (paradise, divine magic).

The operator can use the same name either to evoke or invoke.

The key to every practice is the Immaculate Conception.

As you think, so you evoke; as you conceive, so you create; but the magical act of conception cannot be understood as the result of meditation and lengthy vigils.

In Magic, *conception* is a lightning flash, a dazzling operation of our psyche, which relies on two factors:

1. The most perfect education of the physical and intellectual bodies
2. The will of good and evil

To summarize, I would add:

- that only in an integrated consciousness, outside of any influence of the environment, of superstition or of passion, does the volitional power manifest itself spontaneously without effort, by the simple imaginative act;
- that the imagination is an instrument of creation in integrated consciousnesses;
- that the creation of a form conceived in this inner condition is sufficient for the form to be realized;
- that such achievement is not the result of an effort, but of a state of the independent inner being that knows no obstacle;

- that the realization, *above as below,* is an act of love;
- that this holds both in good and in evil, that is, it occurs both in forms or realities which bring about usefulness and pleasure and in those which bring harm and pain.

Man has great responsibility for his actions in the society in which he lives. He is rewarded or punished by human justice. But the well-known *judgment seat of God* of which Catholics speak really does exist, because every action of the conscience of a living being is cause for life or death, and the incorruptible justice of the equilibrium of Divine Providence rewards or punishes, gives or takes away, in the lives that follow human life, just as in the society of men.

Sins, that is, one's faults, must be brought to account and debts paid. The thief must pay back the man he robbed. *Qui gladio ferit, gladio perit* [He who lives by the sword, must die by the sword].* Christ's chalice must be drunk to the dregs. That is how we must understand the "eye for an eye" of holy books.

Pardon is expiation.

The law of fate is inexorable. Jehovah, who is the just, almighty God, is also the God of fate: *inexorable.*

As you sow, so shall you reap.

If you paint in black, black will be the specter of justice to you.

So Essenism, a mixture of Jewish, Chaldean, and Egyptian science transfused into Catholicism, could not define pardon without invoking the sacrament of penitence. Penitence is expiation, the purification, the washing away of ancient sins. Man creates his happiness and his unhappiness. Karma is the fruit of all our actions: inexorable, inviolable law. To it all men are subject.

The elimination of karma in Buddhism is reached through fasting and abstinence; in Christianity, through purification that works toward its elimination by means of magical self-creation.

---

*[Ancient Latin proverb with a parallel in Matthew 26. —*Ed.*]

Karma is our work, our merit or demerit, because unswerving justice reigns immutably over all the animate and inanimate world.

Every good or bad action must bear fruit: no grace of a personal God can exonerate the malefactor from the consequences of his crime.

Karma is not a force that works from outside like a god, but an inner force that works continually on us. To deny this would be to deny the cause of the law that produces the effect.

But in magic, to admit this would be to deny the creative action of human thought in a man who has reached the state of pure *mag* upon an impure man. If every action is a creation, a form, a different arrangement of molecules of things existing by themselves, a pure spirit can purge an unclean spirit through a creative action, destroying his karma and dissipating his larvae.

Through an action of sincere and penetrative love, karma is changed by the force of penetration.

Hence the need in magic for self-cleansing, which any disciple must achieve, for the purification of his spirit.

Remember, disciple, that if, in the ordinary life of man, every action, every word, or sigh has a reaction in the hyperphysical world, in the magical life of the initiates even a fleeting thought is a creation.

That is why initiation is granted in its fullness only to men of the highest morality, because the danger of prevarication is thus reduced. The responsibility of man before the unseen of his organic life is great, but the responsibility of the initiates is still greater. The masters are jointly responsible with the disciples, when the disciples go wrong, and they are responsible for the bad deeds of the disciples if their punishment of the disciples does not fall upon them like a scourge foreboding Jehovah's inexorability.

In magic, the disciple and his master are jointly *responsible* partners in a contract, as a lawyer might say, and the responsibility of the master is great when he initiates into the high secrets a profane man who may unconsciously violate or prevaricate his mission. Also, direct initiation is always something painful, which the masters avoid.

Christ's pardoning of the flagellant is a very great and glorious work of charity: when the offending act does not generate any revenge for the offense in the offended, divine justice is more clement. But the moral outrage, the monster that some lunatic substitutes for the ideal of magical conception in his obscene operations, represents a scourge, which has reverberations in the invisible world, without any hope of pardon or forgiveness.

Now, he who cannot assume entire responsibility for his own actions is a pupil and cannot be initiated.

He who can assume this responsibility and thinks of and gives life to evil is a monster of madness.

The complete man, aspiring to the Divine Kingdom through universality, is Buddha; the man sacrificing himself to universality to reach God is Christ.

Peace and sacrifice, love and virtue, the ideal and the good, truth and light: this is the magical work I am hastening toward its realization.

To convert this love into determinations of time, place, and individuals is diabolical work and black magic.

Do not begin any work of magic if not from God.

Do not operate without the virtue of purity.

Just as you are pure and diligent, so will your work of magic be rewarded with *fulfillment*.

Ariel comes, intelligence, spirit, daimon, if you are pure, strong, exuberant, powerful, bold, and vital. As the emanation of the high conception, which animates you, he comes down to be embodied in you; your arm is his arm, your mind is his mind, your heart is his heart. You command and he commands, you think and he thinks, you create and he creates.

Turn the action upside down.

Do you want *Ariel,* who is life, creation, victory, and thought, to descend and come for wicked deeds? Do you thirst for power and do you want an age of tyranny to strike? . . . Invoke him in the same way. *Ariel* will not come. It is the spirit of lies that arrives; it is the larva of your wickedness that comes to life in the delirium of your passion.

Magical practice, based on the infinite intelligence of the purest spirits, is opposed to the passionate state of the human heart that aims at wicked deeds of egotism and separation and revenge. All the *spirits* that talk to the minds of bad magicians are only larvae of passions. All the *spirits* that ape the Eternal Father in communications to writing mediums, which incite contempt, separation, and hatred, are only larvae.

When the larvae become monstrous, Asmael, the angel of punishment, arrives, and breaks, shatters, destroys, and . . . you fall in the dust, and pay for this astral violation in madness and premature death.

Let's now come to the practice.

In natural magic, *Ariel* is lord of the elements, as in divine magic; he is intelligence and force.

Natural magic comprises all the operations done by men on the inferior world, on that world that blind men believe to be inanimate and unreasoning. It is natural, that is, acting on *natural* or *created* things; whereas it is divine, or acting on the divine world, when it is applied to the natural world and creates.

The greatest confusion generally comes about when one confuses the two parts of Arcane Wisdom or *Wisdom of the Ark,* and ordinarily the Magician is supposed to be able to act interchangeably on the distinct parts of the Universe* through identical means.

If we apply to man all that I have already explained about the quinary and its astrological relationship, the action of the magician becomes twofold: to command and to pray according to whether he *evokes* created things to himself, or *invokes* divine powers for creation.

Hence, the two supreme powers of the two categories of operations in magic.

To evoke means to call with the voice *to oneself; to invoke* means to call with the voice *in oneself.*

No work of magic begins without invocation, nor must the disciple

---

Uni-verse, Uni-versus, spell and read the *letters.*

begin his real initiation without invoking the *highest principle* or *Christ* within himself.

His physical invocation must correspond to that of his mind.

His invocation in the form of prayer must be the sign of his ascent and the hope for his success.

The operations of divine initiation toward spiritual ascent begin under the influence of *Ariel; Ariel* is the center irradiating force and capacity; he is, in magical language, the guardian and guiding angel.

Now, at this point I think it useful for the disciple, after so much theory, really to try and make a start if he feels like it and, in order to shift his life away from the world of blind profanity to that of light and force, he must practice the twelve magical aphorisms of Iriz ben Assir, a high priest of the Beroso period. These aphorisms of elementary magic have never been published in the Western world and form a part the initiatic books of the Egyptian Rite. The neophytes to this order are given the twelve aphorisms and are advised to learn them by heart. In expounding these twelve aphorisms, translating them from the original hieratical Syrian—that is, from the ideographs of the period in which the college of Eastern priests bequeathed them to posterity—I have adapted them to the intelligence of modern people and will add comments as clear *as I am allowed to give.* Through the study and practice of the laws of these magical aphorisms, which are a synthesis of what is needed to become a priest, the disciple who has followed me up to now can begin his own education.

THE APHORISMS

First Aphorism
One is the world, one is man, and one is the egg. The world, the man, and the egg make three. In each *one* you see *three,* in the world, in man, and in the egg you find *three* times *three.*

If you want to learn the secret of the egg, reach for *three.*

If you want to understand the mystery of man, raise yourself to *six.*

If you want the intuition of the great arcanum of the world, go up to *nine*.

Inhale and exhale *three* times in order to know the secret of the egg.

Six times for the mystery of man, *nine* times for the arcanum of the world.

So Ea (Jehovah) created first the world, then man, and then the egg and gave the last the secret both of man and the world.

So, my son, the first aphorism of sacred and hidden things is in the number 369. Without light, without noise, without any thought whatsoever which is not aspiration to Ea, bury yourself alive with your ears stopped with beeswax and lamb's wool in a cave where no earthly light comes in, and there inhale and exhale *369* until you see the World in the Egg of Ea.

Second Aphorism

When creating the world, Ea contemplated two things, white and black, hot and cold, and his breath became cold and hot and he gave his hot breath to man and his cold breath to woman, because the former was to kindle and to heat and the latter was to take and to preserve; so you, my son, as soon as you saw the world of Ea, "learned" what *life* is and how life is *blown* from the world of Ea to the world of the egg; and you will discover that the life of male things is not the life of female things, and that only into things having a double nature did Ea blow twice.

So, the second aphorism you must remember is that you cannot do a divine work without a knowledge of the life-nature in the egg, in man, and in the world of Ea.

Third Aphorism

Once you have learned to inhale and exhale, to distinguish the life-nature of males and females in the things of the world of Ea, you must learn to blow, as Ea did in the world, on the egg of things not yet created. Then go back into your *living sepulcher,* stop up your ears again, and instead of inhaling and exhaling, blow *369* times on the things you feel but do not see. *While blowing, puff up your cheeks, do not puff up your belly, otherwise the breath will go back where it originated, and you will die.* My son, if you practice this rule you will find out how blowing *into the sky,** you light the *fire (pyr).*

Fourth Aphorism

If you have learned how to know the world of Ea, the life of the *double breath* and how to light, by blowing (*insufflating*), the fire in heaven, you will take yourself to the highest mountain in your country, *and you will sit on the naked ground putting a fruit tree on the right and a seed on the left.* Blowing on the tree, you will dry up the tree as if it were struck by the wind of Schen (the desert) and insufflating on the seed you will remake the tree. Then from the ground you will see a two-headed serpent emerge and with two voices[†] he will say to you: First, "I am the seed"; second, "I am the tree." Then you will understand that as the two heads have only one trunk, so the seed and the tree are but one; then you will dry up the new tree and the new seed and will ask Ea to teach you. Light the fire with your breath, and Ea will talk to you from the flames.

Fifth Aphorism

As soon as Ea has talked to you, his spirit, the giant Egs (Arie), will begin to raise the *winds* around you. These winds are the source of your power, of your force and your light; but beware of entrusting yourself wholly to them, because Ea and his spirit Egs are stronger than you, and you would die if you were raised alive to where man cannot live.

Sixth Aphorism

Build yourself a ship[‡] with a sail that the wind of Egs cannot rend, and as soon as you see the wind swelling the waters and the waters mount-

---

*[*Cielo* (Italian), from the Latin *coelum,* meaning the sky or heaven, and what is hidden or occult. —*Trans.*]
†That is, with a voice from each head.
‡The ark; here we come to the flood.

ing to the sky, go into the ship and say to Egs: "Take me where the waters cannot reach me." Then the water will be swollen by seven spirits of Egs.*

Fou—pushes
Xi—redirects
Mne—sustains
Ag—leads
Mor—holds
Mō—hears and speaks
Rā—sees

On the fortieth day you will feel the ship touch land.

Mō will say: "The water recedes."
Rā will see the top of a triangular mountain.

Then, to know the truth, change yourself into a black bird and fly, and you will find the corpses and carcasses that will enchain you. Go back in spirit to your ship and change yourself into a dove and thank Ea, then Egs continues to rotate and you will make the waters swell and recede as you like and you will know the second spirit, Ise.

My prose, when it seems obscure and I cannot make it more explicit, will serve as a signpost to the mysterious way of him who practices and who will understand in time how and when he is in the conditions I am touching upon.

• ◆ •

First, I will say a few things that are more congenial to the modern age, and then I will follow them with the comments of Bne Aagar (perhaps a priest of a later period than Beroso or perhaps, more exactly, the name of a school or sect).

It seems to me that I hear people say: "You, Maestro Kremmerz,

---

*In the ideograph the spirit is represented by a dove, from which comes the Holy Spirit or Dove of the Catholic Church.

want to teach us the practice through six aphorisms out of the nine you promised, but although you may comment on them at great length, we are quite sure you are not going to give us the explanation of such obscurities as clearly as we should like to have it. You will always direct us to philosophical reflections rather than to the practice we should like to grasp, in order to see miracles occur."

I answer this by summing up in a few words what I have scattered and repeated in previous pages, intending to warn the public about occult truths. I say and repeat to my reader and disciple: "If you think that by reading books of occult philosophy you can pluck from the air the *Secretum Secretorum* of Universal Magic, you are deluding yourself: don't waste your time, wits, and money. For you, books of magic will be a 'book of abstract poetry' full of blue horizons and full of illusions. You can never set your foot into the house of truth in any way if the vague thinking does not match the action."

Thought is faith and is religious.

Action is magic and is science.

Do not believe anything just through hearsay; do not believe in traditions that come down to us tired and distorted by human tongues; do not believe in anything just because men talk a lot about it; nor should you believe only because the testimony of a wise man is given to you; do not believe in anything just because probabilities are in its favor or because through habit you deem it true; do not believe in the sole authority of your master and priest. Take as the truth, and live according to it, only what your research and your experience prove is good for your health, your welfare, and for the welfare of other men like you.

Hieratical science, I am telling you, was and is considered by common men either as an illusion or a faith, while to the initiate it must never cease being *consciousness*. Blind faith is becoming to the masses, and is part of religion for the profane. On the contrary, faith as the result of one's own research, after the research has proved its truth, is hieratical science and priestly consciousness.

Never say "Magister dixit," because in this case you will have faith in his science, but not consciousness, and your duty to become an initiate is to possess and conquer the latter through active work under the guidance of the initiator.

The man who thinks, aspires, like the Christian believer who recites the Lord's Prayer, to the coming of the kingdom of the Father.

The man who practices, accomplishes, like the *Father*, the *kingdom's work.*

If my reader wants to become a student of magic, he must start practicing—that is, acting—and before acting he must educate himself, and before educating himself he must *understand*.

So, *to understand, to educate oneself, to act:* here are the three pivots in the early practice of magic.

In the first part I explained how he who is so lucky as to find a master can receive from him *vivissimo animo et brevi tempore* [in the most lively spirit and in a short time] all that can be useful for his ascent.

To *understand:* in the presentation of divine secrets do not take the words literally, but consider the intention or spirit *behind* them. Christ's parables are, like the history of the Jewish migrations, full of struggles and rules, in which each man's name expresses a spirit of action, and each word of battle hints at the conflict of spirit and profane form. The angels are taciturn but active: they speak very little but their actions speak loud. The actions are the work of God; deeds are the language of the spirits of God. Words, speeches, grammatical discourse* belong to the mob and make men similar to beasts that need their voices to express their needs. That's why *grammarians,* experts in human language and discourse, were highly disparaged by the philosophers of ancient times who flourished from the Orphic and Pythagorean schools of the temples sacred to truth.

Subjective silence, or not speaking, places the individual outside any artificial stasis of autonomous creations.

---

*Grammata, the spoken word.

The words we pronounce are the confirmation of our own ideas repeatedly realized by means of articulated sounds.

Men who talk a lot condense notions that they have not yet physically digested. He who does not believe, but says, ends up believing what he says.

Education in inner and personal silence is the best psychical preparation for the separation of the heavier body from the three superior elements.

There is no initiation that does not begin with silence: do not speak of what you will know or of what you will see, and keep silent not just with your mouth, the organ for transmission of thought. Education in silence, by mechanical irradiation, influences the lunar sensibility of the soul, and the latter will learn to be silent, as a closed mouth is silent.

Everything must be silent around him who sets out to conquer his reintegration, so that his solar intelligence may be manifest in him: it must be silent subjectively and objectively, with the mouth, in action and in thoughts, while sleeping or waking, because he who speaks creates, and each creation is a displacement of form and, consequently, an occultation of primitive amorphous truth, or the spirit of light.

The disciple must know how to keep silent and live in the midst of the crowd that is easily influenced, but which does not influence the wise man, whose soul must be insensible to all words, noises, and customs, which are the main influences upon men. And that is not all: he must keep silent with his soul and compel all the spirits who speak to it to be silent also.

If the disciple can keep silent with his soul and his mouth, and live isolated in the world, completely alone in the midst of the milling crowd who preaches falsehoods, he will hear the voice of the Master in his spirit and not simply in sound.

The first aphorism says: *One is the world, one is man, and one is the egg. The world, the man, and the egg make three.*

If *one* is the world, the man and the egg are in the *world.* The *logos,* or word of the absolute idea, is unique in the world, in man, and in the egg.

Therefore, the same language of facts and phenomena, which represents the evolutionary series of the universal mind One, includes the language of facts and phenomena of the two unities of the subcategory:

One = the world
One = man
One = the egg

But that is not enough: the laws explaining the first Unity are analogous to the others: the egg is the spirit because it is a germ, as man is a creature because he is the outcome of the germ of the laws of universal Unity, and the world is God because he is the language of the Universal Mind.

He who wants to begin to *understand,* he who wants to get hold of the first keys to the occult treasure of the sciences that form the patrimony of the Magicians, must get rid of the whole baggage of profane ideas in order to enter the world of causes, through a synthetic and not analytical process, which is the real and great enigma of sacred mysteries.

One is the law, one the existence of all things, one is the matrix of any perceptible form, and beyond this single truth there is nothing but reasoning folly, which has come up with the idea that imperfect man must hope for everything by grace and that the eternal life of the spirits passes beyond the power of matter which is the single law, the single essence, the single matrix of what is, was, and will be forever on earth and for all the stars in the firmament.

To those preparing for initiation: *One is life;* quartz, a rose, a beautiful woman, a hideous man are but the production of the same germ of the life of the universe.

Has the universe got a soul? It is the same soul that keeps the atoms of quartz together, that colors and withers the petals of a rose, that makes a woman convulse under the spasm of desire, and that makes a man repugnant.

Has the universe got a mind? It is the same mind that manifests itself in different levels of intelligence, in minerals, vegetables, animals.

What exists for the common man, stranger to the intuition of Hermetic unity? Nothing but words.

What exists for the student of occultism? Only one thing: unity in the most expansive expression of the phenomena of nature.

The first aphorism states this law as the fundamental axiom.

This is the key to any analogy in the science of the spirit and in religions. If the disciple *does not understand this, he will never understand* what astrology is for magicians, and he will say it is a superstition (i.e., ignorance that inspires faith, as Bonaventura Tondi wrote in the *Rivulus Sapientiae,* 1681); he will neither understand the spirit of alchemy, nor that of evocations, nor the other of universal love and of the ideal of unity aspiring to God as a return and as an end.

But you will try in vain to understand, my reader, if you want to find, expressed in common grammar, the clear *intention* that animates the magical doctrinal expositions of men who have the power to transmit and preserve the secret of action—the Golden Fleece of Jason's voyages, the Troy of the Greek wars, and the building of Rome (Urbis) of the Latenda Saturnia!

In magic, to *understand* is to *conquer.*

Ordinarily, men who have the power to perceive the occult truths in scientific expositions of Magic (true *poems* in the classical sense of the word) feel themselves driven to the attempt, by one of those *lights,* not properly appreciated by common people who took the form of gods, angels, heroes, and spirits of the dead according to the times. And this *light* speaks to the mind of the disciple and says to him: "try, see, touch, and you will succeed." But if this *light* is wedded to man's pride, it becomes false, and he enters the labyrinth of the Minotaur, a blind alley, long, winding, at the end of which there is folly, death, and dissolution.

How many people start properly and finish disastrously when they study the science of the magicians? Why? Because they think they understand, but they fail to comprehend. The invisible world speaks the immutable language of unities, which they do not understand: they mix it with their pride and fall into Gehenna (*obscurissimi loci diaboli domum* [to the home of the most obscure devil's place], says B. Tondi) from which they emerge completely destroyed.

Orientalists and theosophists, researchers into established methods and formulae of religions, have from time to time affirmed that the principle on which magical ascent is based is pride: the *ego* or *logos* springs only from the complete and independent intelligent unity. This is true only in the outer form. If you reflect on the fact that *every religious and monastic order in all the religions of the World is, as in invisible nature, based on hierarchy and obedience;* that the higher spirits, capable of a complete ascent, have appeared and appear in every order of the various religions; that in *hierarchy* and *obedience* the independent Unities are formed without imbalance; then, it will be clear that you are in the wrong if, in Magic, you think you can separate brother from brother, fellow from fellow, disciple from master, to create the satanic synagogue of disagreement and division, generating terrible passions of hatred that impede the progress of spirit in the highest zone of truth.

Read the parable of the prodigal son.

This happens between master and disciple, as I know from experience. The son takes his father's wealth and goes far away to use it up in revelry; he supposes that he can find everywhere what he had from his father.

One fine morning, when the would-be sage would least like to admit it, the prodigal must recognize that he is less than nothing, that the wealth is gone, that everything has crumbled around him.

The *Light,* or a *light,* appears in the disciple's soul and tells him: study, comprehend, work, love. In study, comprehension, work, and love he must embrace the whole invisible and visible world.

The *Light* urges him toward a spring where he can quench his thirst for truth. He walks with apprehension; he tastes and says as the biblical God after the creation of water, *et vidit hoc bonum esse* [and he saw that it was good]. Then the *Light* comforts him, and he shows himself in the blue waters of the lake. Then man's pride comes into play and the spirit of the earth, which the Bible symbolizes in the Serpent, and which Jewish Kabbalists symbolize in Samiel and Astaroth, whispers to him insistently: *you will navigate deep waters and not drown,* and seduces him.

What forms the mental *Unity of the Logos* in the initiate? The divine Light or the spirit of the earth? Obedience or pride? The spirit of the Universe or the breath of the beast?

This is why, in the present state of civilization of various so-called civilized peoples, really advanced men are rare, apart from within the most austere orders of various religions. In profane social life, man does not pass the test of the serpent of the earth and falls into his jaws.

The serpent has the face of a woman or a nice young man; it enchants when it speaks. It puts you to sleep if it breathes; it makes you happy if it hisses. But it inexorably kills any man who entrusts himself to it completely, perpetually, unconditionally.

Those who begin have a false understanding when the spirit of the earth predominates in them. It is the spirit of obedience and love that is essentially divine.

If you reflect on all the puns and sophisms that the individual spirit of pride can make when talking of obedience and love, you will understand how catastrophic it is to force your own interpretations upon them.

And I should like my patient reader *now and forever to fully understand* the spirit of these things, which I am simplifying for him, so that he may eat the roses and see Isis glowing with immortal beauty.

•◆•

To educate yourself and to practice: How do you educate yourself and what do you practice?

When the education of the disciple of magic is not started or completed by a master, it must be based on the comprehension of symbols and of the science explained above. If the comprehension is mistaken, magical education will also be mistaken. It must follow tendencies toward *unity in the disciple:* that is to say, following the synthesis of his aspirations and potentiality.

How do you practice?

Here is the problem.

Will you start from the egg or germ and ascend to the world, or will you start from the world and descend to the germ?

Start from the spiritual germ, and set yourself a fixed and immutable aim; think that you must reach this aim, whatever it be, as long as it is honest and moral.

In order to thoroughly study the means to educate your will, never change your aim. Before choosing it you can consider it as much as you like, but after choosing it, never shrink from your objective.

If you have *understood* the first aphorism, study the germ. Educate yourself to plumb the unknown depths of your spirit for the breath, which will bring about your transformation—and the Light will appear to you.

It is a mistake for anyone who begins to want to see the outcome of the operations he has done, even in a very trivial form, overnight: forget it. The realization often comes after endless painful years.

I teach my disciples in Magic a truth immutable in all times, in all countries, truth beyond speech: *don't deceive yourself; words change like men's moods, bow only to truth whatever its name, whatever it's called; truth is one.* Jesus Christ, philosophical conscience, the higher Self, Buddha* are but the divine principle in us. Talk to yourself and to Jesus Christ as Thomas à Kempis wanted; look for the angel contained in your own body, as the mystics say. For you it is all the same, because it is

---

*Personally, I don't think Western civilization needs to get involved in the sacred terminology and theology of Indian Brahmanism to determine forces, intelligences, and divinities, which in Greco-Latin paganism and in Egyptian antiquity we find represented in symbols that are more poetic and more congenial to European sensibilities. If Europeans have no wish to extend their studies beyond their ancestors' knowledge, it is sufficient for them to examine, understand, and explain Catholic symbolism, a worthwhile study for all disciples of Magic.

not words that make truth, rather truth is *betrayed* by the words of men who, after betraying it, are no longer able to call it by its name.

Let's read the first aphorism again.

One is the world, one is man, and one is the egg; the world, the egg, and man make three.

So the magician must perceive within himself the three component parts of his individuality:

The *world* corresponds to the whole of human sensibility, which is in contact with outer or profane society.

Thomas à Kempis says: *Ista est summa per contemptum mundi tendere ad regna coelestia.* That is, despise the world and you will get to Heaven.

What is this world that we must despise?

The senses: vanity of vanities, *vanitas vanitatum,* says the officiating monk. The world is matter, the sensations of matter, the illusion of material effluvium, spiritually unredeemed human society, pride, ambition, the satisfaction of carnal desires. This world of the Egyptian priesthood was called in the Middle Ages the *sublunary world,* that is, variable or mutable as the moon; there can be no *immaculate conception* without putting the *sublunary world* or the *moon* under the feet. So the world is within us: it is that part of us that feels earthly effluvia more strongly, it is the most earthly, the most socially brutal part of *Homo sapiens.*

Man corresponds to the second-degree sensibility of the thinking individual. Beyond physical sensibility in developed—so-called civilized—individuals, a hyperphysical sensibility becomes evident. In the thinking individual, *man* manifests himself only in human mentality, active in society.

Thomas à Kempis says, therefore, try to take your heart away from visible things in order to turn all your feelings toward the invisible. *Man* becomes manifest in us only when mentality is advanced, that is, when the lower sensibility disappears. Those who are recognized as geniuses by contemporary society are only men, mentally developed and advanced. Intellect has its human explication in the society where it lives as a body, the society that was called *humanitas,* from *humus,* "soil," the origin of *homo.* The second term of the first magical aphorism is made of three terms, the highest of which is still *humanus,* that is, *earthly,* though it seems divine to mortals.

These three terms of mentality are:

$$
Man \left\{ \begin{array}{l} \textit{Reason} \\ \textit{Will} \\ \textit{Inspiration} \end{array} \right.
$$

Inspiration, which is commonly considered as a principle of divine manifestation in human mentality, is, as I said, only apparently so. We might say *in-spiration,* a kind of entwining of the spirit with itself, and rather than representing the divine term incarnate in man, it represents the highest evolution of the human mind.

This human inspiration in magic is represented by the symbol of the moon, because as the moon has the power to reflect the light of Osiris upon the earth and thereby govern our world, so each human inspiration comes as a reflected beam of divine truth.

The student, who philosophically studies the secret of the source of the human imagination, can draw a very subtle application of the beams of light reflected on us by a mirror, and has the true comprehension of lunar potentiality.

What does a crystal surface on which a ray of sun is reflected do? It reflects the same ray weakened, wavering, and diminished in a different direction to give light, albeit with its weakened, wavering, and diminished light, to invisible objects. So it is with the moon, to which human inspiration belongs, which is the earthly vision of things with a light that seems divine, but is human.

In comparison to men, women are lunar; in comparison to the master, the disciple is lunar; in comparison to absolute truth, any relative truth is lunar.

The *egg* or germ must be understood as the deepest root of the soul *known* to man; in other words it is the Jesus Christ of Thomas à Kempis, that is, the highest and purely divine principle existing in man.

The means are two and the ways several.

The passive ascetic or religious life is the easiest and the longest.

The active initiatic or magic life is the shortest, that is, the fastest. But in nature everything is evolution and everything proceeds by degrees; rapidity does not mean the suppression of intermediate stages, but the condensation of periods. Consequently, greater are the pains, bloodier the wounds, and more tremendously sharp the crown of thorns.

Theologians teach Catholics that the *Son of Man* suffered the pains of the body but that the Son of God could neither suffer nor agonize.

Now, the Son of Man ends in the spasms of Calvary, which will bring about the Resurrection of the Son of God.

This is the symbolism of Easter Sunday, which reminds us of symbols that are older than the Psalter, such as eggs or lambs, the patient and innocent martyrs of a deep evolutive mystery, the truth and intelligence of which has not dawned on the people ignorant of sacred mysteries.

You do not reach the *seed* if first you have not destroyed the *world* in the individual and have not voluntarily made the sacrifice of love of the *soul* (man) to the divine principle. Once you have understood this principle, you will easily understand the meaning of the sacrament of Communion according to the orthodox Christian ritual. The faithful should reach the knowledge of Christ; that is, according to the prime principle, they should be in contact with the *divine Self* as *Truth* and *Absolute Light* common to all men who believe in Christ.* But in practice, my dear disciple, only a few men, who above all constitute human priesthood, are already close to the nirvana that frightens individualists so much, and are in contact with the divine Self or Jesus Christ; that is why the cult had to *magically* make use of communion with

---

*I am the way, the truth, and the life.

unleavened bread and the sanctified host so that the *same Christ* (of which the host and the bread represent the *realization*), consecrated in a symbol, may be taken by all the faithful who are actually still very far from the *true* Christ.

• ◆ •

To sum up, the trinitary form is the dogmatic foundation of the religion of Christ in its magic-symbolic expression of Catholicism; all this is magic in doctrine and practice.

Catholicism divides man into three elements:

1. Body
2. Soul
3. Divine Spirit or Christ

The *body* is the world and is symbolized in the Devil or the rule of the senses and passions, or *Hell.*

The *soul* is the mentality and is symbolized in the gradual purification of thinking man until the highest point of his development, which corresponds to *Purgatory.*

The *Spirit,* or *Christ,* is the divine Self or the Son of God made man, the vision of whom is *Paradise.*

Hence we infer that Hell, Purgatory, and Paradise are within ourselves and that we are eternal in matter, in human spirit, and in the Kingdom of Christ.

Spiritualists call these three components of the reasoning being:

1. Body
2. Peri-spirit or soul
3. Pure Spirit

But magic in its theosophy, which is always concerned with the teaching of occult truth in man, states that the predominance of one of these parts in man may be at different levels and says: the *world* or the *material body* corresponding to the least developed individual is *instinctive;* corresponding to a more advanced individual, it is *discerning* good from evil for its impressive sensual consequences; and corresponding to a still more advanced individual, it is *reasoning.*

All modern studies of criminality should be the experimental field for the three material elements in the body of the individual dedicated to brutal sensuality. All the seven sins, which the Catholic Church calls *deadly,* enumerate the different instinctive forms of the brutality of the human body.

The sexual union becomes possible only as a *sacrament,* that is, as the sanctification of the infernal act whose excuse is the union of two *souls.* Beware that it is not the union between *two* spirits, because for the Christians one is the spirit of God, that is, the Holy Spirit, and the incarnation of the Holy Spirit is *Christ.* The communion of two souls in a single soul cemented by love is concrete in its shared inspiration and enjoyment of Paradise.

Now:

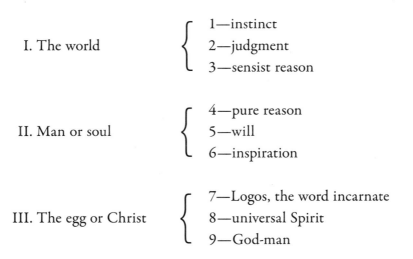

I. The world
- 1—instinct
- 2—judgment
- 3—sensist reason

II. Man or soul
- 4—pure reason
- 5—will
- 6—inspiration

III. The egg or Christ
- 7—Logos, the word incarnate
- 8—universal Spirit
- 9—God-man

In this very short, concise synthesis you can see the three number 3s of the first magical aphorism, and everyone will understand these nine steps on the way to divinizing man, a divinization that is accomplished not in a nine-year university or high-school course but over a long span of years, by rising above worldliness and humanity.

•◆•

To sum up again: many spiritualist mediums who believe they are in communication with spirits no longer incarnate *very often* are in contact, at the most, only with *inspiration* (no. 6) of the soul stage, and often they speak only with their *will,* unconsciously acting on *inspiration.*

As for dreams: all ordinary dreams of a sensory origin belong to the world; *symbolic dreams* belong to the lunar or inspirative zone and must be interpreted well in order to understand their truth.

Only the higher initiate and certain saints (not all of them) have the prerogative of speaking the language of truth with the superior principle of the divine Self and of knowing *what is.*

Anyway, in dreams certain men who have not yet reached a very high degree of development may have, by true *grace* or by efficient virtue of the divine will, the inspirative glimpse, without symbols, of truth; but also these dreams and these men are rare, and are essentially prophetic.

•◆•

To sum up again: in order to practice the magical life, you must have a definite objective ahead of you. Say to yourself: *"I want science,"* or *"I want virtue,"* or *"I want riches,"* and try to refer your ideal to one of the three magical elements of the first aphorism.

Science belongs to the divine principle, virtue to mentality, riches to the world.

You will obtain science evolving toward your highest divine principle; virtue, by practicing it; and riches . . . by dominating them.

Allow me a digression.

Many people want to study magic to acquire riches. In fact, of all the secrets the easiest is how to become rich.

Riches represent provision beyond individual needs: of a philosopher who feeds on a crumb of bread and lives in a barrel, and of a millionaire who works and robs his fellow men to increase his patrimony, the philosopher is the richer.

Before wishing for riches, one must clarify what one wants: do you want them to satisfy your life's necessities? This is refused only to those who have to expiate errors and sins still uncleansed. Providence is a truth that all just, patient, and faithful men have experienced.

The Lord governs his children with two angels: one brings bread, the other honey. Let the just man who is without bread in a field where revelers and rich people disport themselves, never utter the curse: "God has forgotten me." Let him pray and he will have. If it comes late, there is a providential reason that makes him experience the pangs of hunger. God does not forget, because the spirit of God in us is deaf only when we bury it under our lies.

The disciple in magic *must not* desire in prayer; desiring is contrary to all magical realizations. That is how the false adepts of magic die in despair, without grace and virtue, because *they desired before obtaining grace.*

The disciple in magic sets out his need to God and asks for its fulfillment *if it is right to have it.* You have no bread; you have no roof; perhaps it is written in the principle of absolute justice that you must suffer hunger in order to redeem yourself.

At the beginning of *Il Mondo Secreto* I warned not to confuse passive religion with active magic. The practice of magic is the scientific application of the religious theory that is fodder for the masses: to magic can be ascribed, by virtue (*vir:* man or active), only those beings who are capable of dominating the tide of passivity, which, in symbolism, is represented by the moon.

Magical practice—I have repeated this many times—can be followed either by those natures who are aristocratically positive or those with supremely inflexible wills or by persons who want and feel that it is possible to arrive, not by praying to God, which is something everyone does, but by identifying oneself with the divine active nature and merging it with one's own will illuminated by justice.

Not all have the necessary perseverance for this second self-creation over the span of one earthly life by means of the wise practices of magic; rather, only a few people are capable of working incessantly in our art over the long span of one existence, being guided by the instinct for research on transformation so as to prepare not only their spiritual ascent but also the continuity of their own existence.

The occult forces residing in us, integrated into the powers that belong essentially to our animal nature, like the muscles of our body, become atrophied if they are not developed and made elastic by exercise.

The will that directs these forces is a reflection of the divine spark that is our intellect.

Between magic and religion the difference is enormous.

I am speaking to those, that is, to intelligent and young students, who will not be scandalized and confused if I say clearly that magic is *the art and the science of making the active man a god and not compelling him to suffer the ebb and flow of the inconstant tides of the religious moon.*

Let no one who hears me be surprised: these words, which may seem bold at the time in which I write, will live long, and the ideas I am sowing will come to fruition when their time is ripe.

The *Mondo Secreto* may end. Dr. Kremmerz may cease writing and return to the Kingdom of Heaven, but *not one syllable of this truth will be cancelled!* And the forty centuries separating us from the temples of Ur, Babylon, Assyria, Nineveh handed down the political priesthood's true dictate to the resurrection of the judging dead, when the masses, on account of their psychical imperfections and their lack of evolution, could not yet aspire to even know what the priests were about in the depths of their sacred laboratories.

Nothing is new under the sun, but the new element in the mystery of this truth, which cannot be fed to imperfect natures in this period, which prepares better centuries for mankind in transformation, is the divulgation of a dogma that is truth; the new part lies in the perception of this truth by men of different origins and natures, backgrounds and antecedents, characters and thoughts.

We are on the eve of the great scientific revolution that unbelieving scientists, researchers in bacteria, do not expect. We are at a psychical moment of mankind's development in which the memory of so many centuries sleeping under the sepulcher of oblivion is awakening the consciousness of the masses. We are playing the trumpet, which will sound the apocalyptic call of the elected spirits in the memory of the preceding consciousness, and the sun will shine on the nature-soul of the psychical cycle, and the kingdom of Christ will be a thing of the past.

To unite in marriage the two serpents, the invisible one that represents Hermetic sense in its integration, to the visible one, which proceeds from the profane research for the conquest of human knowledge, is a formidable task that takes on the vague and cloudy aspect of utopia.

I am not revealing an ancient secret; I am just setting out a program of research and clearing the clouds that cover the simplicity of the formula.

The Messiah who is to arrive at the beginning of the twentieth century is the link that will unite faith and science and give science the direction of the faith of the masses.

I cannot wholly modernize old magical terms. That will be the work of others who come after me. What I have undertaken to do is to spread the word that the magic of the magicians included all the absolute laws, that is, the schematic laws of the existing material and spiritual order, and that its practice created the sage or magician.

In order to do this, I cannot proceed without illustrating the ancient formulae and without using them. I am taking a step ahead: I am trying to bring together, around this science, some students who do not feel the pressing urge to deny anything a priori.

Once the school (not a sect, because science is not a conspiracy) has been established, its John the Evangelist will come later, but he will have to say: "We are children of the magicians, and magic was the wisdom of the Ark; therefore, truth is one; we are returning to ancient knowledge using new forms."

More I cannot say, because to say more would mean to give away to my readers the secret source of my knowledge, which must be known only to the initiates into the occult truth of the scientific temples of contemporary society.

However, what I have asserted so far, what I have explained, should make it clear to the readers that other things are hidden under the scientific veil of strange lines that go beyond ordinary spiritualism in its revelation of the poetic souls wandering in limbo waiting for a medium who can make them talk to their still-living relatives.

In order to continue with the comments on the aphorisms by Iriz ben Assir, we must understand that, as is said in the first of them, the creator is Ea, and that the disciple in priestly science can only find and begin his purely magical and active education in number 3, the egg. This egg, I said, corresponds to the Christ of religious Catholics, but the search for Christ is not the search for a state of the Spirit, as taught by the Buddhist propagators of insufficiently detailed doctrines, but a complex of relationships connected to the manifestation of the *third state* of the incarnate being.

This third state is reachable and conquerable; but where the work becomes titanic is in the ascent from number 7 to number 9 from the mirror of truth that I presented on page 168. The neophyte without fear, without trembling, without terror, with a very strong will to reach it, passing through the infinite graveyard of human passions and sorrows, reaches the gates of the convoluted Logos (no. 7) and believes himself a god, whereas he is only on the threshold of divinity.

A beautiful Oriental saga tells of Etana* who made a pact with the Eagle of the Sun God that he would be carried to the heaven of Anna.†

So it came about that embracing the Eagle, he rose into space. And

---

*Orientalists read our hierograms wrongly. Eāt: *t,* the final letter of the hierogram, represents Eā dead, that is, fallen.
†The woman without menstruation, like Saint Anne, who without menstruation gave birth to the Virgin Mary, in her turn mother without the participation of the male!

they reached the heaven of Anna. Etana resisted: the earth looked like a speck in space, the sea like a rivulet. But the Eagle suggested that they should continue upward to visit the Morning Star (the goddess Venus) and resumed his flight. When they were about to reach there, Etana looked down and said, "Stop, I cannot go on"; the divine bird immediately descended . . . but Etana fell down dead because his masculine strength had failed him.

And yet the neophyte is only a magician at the feet of Isis once he has eaten the roses with which old Apuleius's rehumanized ass was decorated.

But in the first aphorism it is said that Ea made the world first, then man, and then the egg; this conceals not the system of creation but the phase of development of Divine Intelligence in the animal body. *Inhale and exhale three times,* says the first aphorism, in order to know the secret of the egg. This "inhale" means to draw the spirit into yourself; "exhale" means to let it out; this is a completely Oriental form to express the attracting and repelling act of the generation of the intelligent principle.

But the second aphorism hints at and develops the method of creating magic potency.

On creating the world, Ea contemplated two things (says Iriz ben Assir): *white and black, hot and cold, and his breath became cold and hot, and he gave the hot breath to man and the cold breath to woman,* and so on.

1. Is there an essential difference between *active life* (male) and *passive life* (female)?
2. Once we have put it that the two kinds of *life* are different, and reflected upon it, can a woman become a magician?

I will answer briefly, but what I am going to say cannot be clearly understood by everyone in its real meaning, and in its application to the practice. And I am referring to what I said in the first part.

1. The *one* vital current divides, and realizes itself separately.

2. Both men and women can become powerful magicians if men awaken the female faculties in themselves and vice versa.

As for the expression *to blow life* as used in the second aphorism, the *blowing* is taken here as a symbol of emanation. Blessed are those in whom Ea has blown twice. The two souls in the same individual intertwine in love, like the serpents on Mercury's caduceus, and they sing divine fruitfulness.

From this we can understand what the ancient initiated priests meant when they said to the disciple: bury yourself alive with your ears stopped with beeswax and lambs' wool in a hole where no worldly light can enter, and there inhale and exhale, until you achieve the vision of the world of Ea. In the very powerful exercise of attracting and repelling the spirit of the world, the silent and sleeping virtues of the forces accumulated and reproduced in universal life are awakened.

Isolation, moral improvement, the awakening of your occult and hidden nature: this is the simple, literal translation of priestly doctrine.

• ◆ •

A scientifically perfect man is neither all body nor all spirit, *but the integration of the powers of the spirit in the body that feeds it and serves all its manifestations in a constant equilibrium so as to prevent its unity from any prevarication of the two factors of which it is composed.*

To speak more clearly: a man who lives in a state of exuberance of the soul is imperfect, just as imperfect as a man who vegetates by drowning in the flesh the rights of the soul.

Here it is necessary to understand the constitution of man. Man must be considered as a being containing in himself the four elements that constitute the universe:

1. A sensitive and solid body (flesh, bones, tissues).
2. A subtler emanation deriving from the above, which makes up his lower sensibility (nerves, nerve centers, brain).

3. A more complete individuality deriving from the two above, which constitutes his mentality (mental man).

4. A luminous intellective principle, which takes part in universal life and is therefore an inexhaustible fount of vitality, both spiritual and corporeal.

The names that Magic gives to these four constituent elements are traditional and borrowed from mythology.

1. *Saturnian* body: it eats, devours, renews, and reproduces itself.

2. *Lunar* body: it reflects the above as the moon reflects the light of the sun.

3. *Mercurial* body, the resulting individuality: mental man with wings at his head and his feet.

4. *Solar* body: the divine individuality that does not manifest itself to man except through the mercurial body, which, in turn, manifests itself to the lunar body and this latter to the saturnian body.

The disciple must understand that this division is made in order that we understand each other in concrete terms, but it does not really exist in man, because these four bodies are interrelated in such a way that every cell, every atom of the human physical body contains the other three rudimentarily or atomically.

Therefore, man in his unity and synthesis is the result of two extremes: the *physical saturnian body,* which absorbs from the earth and from the purely physical sensations with which it is in contact the education and ways of life that are closest to it; and the *solar body,* the opposite pole that takes part in the highest life not only of the earth but of the whole universe composed of the infinite worlds making up the planetary systems known and unknown to astronomers.

Human (*humus* = *terra* = earth) or terrestrial ideas from the physical senses pass to the store of nervous centers, through the nerves that are the vehicles of the saturnian sensibility. The ideas and divine knowledge (God or Zeus, the thunderbolt), that is, the ideas from the vast and grandiose field unknown to the saturnian body, come to us from the highest or solar individuality by means of the mind or mental and mercurial mechanism.

If the lowest sensations dominate, the way to highest perceptions is cut off, and, vice versa, if the solar or divine spiritual principle dominates, the saturnian body is insufficient to preserve the functions of physical life.

The equilibrium of the four elements is represented as a true and real personality, which takes part both in terrestrial and universal Life, and which corresponds to the Christ of the Catholics, the Hermes of the Greeks, and the Mercurius of the philosophers.

Therefore, human integration begins to appear and to progress step-by-step as Hermes appears and progresses in man. Therefore, Hermes is a divine entity if you consider it as the most perfect type of equilibrium between the two binomials:

$$\frac{Saturnian}{Lunar} \quad Hermes \quad \frac{Mercurial}{Solar}$$

This would correspond to the beatifying and balanced state of light that predisposes us to the knowledge of the secrets of all that exists.

The mythical priesthood said that Mercurius or Hermes was born of Maya, the daughter of Atlantis (who wanted to discover the secret of Olympus), and Jupiter (the king of heaven) to indicate the participation of the Hermetic mind at the two extremes, and the Supreme, that is, universal, God gave him wings at his head and feet to execute his orders quickly in heaven and on the earth.

This means that this state of lucid mental equilibrium (Hermetic and mercurial) has a divine and a terrestrial origin, but acts in the Divinity incomprehensible to the common masses and in practical life on earth.

Therefore, the disciple must understand Hermes as the source of pure, integrating, and infallible science, because it sees in the relative finite and the absolute infinite.

Do not be confused: I did not say four parts, but four bodies, each of which is the sublimation of the lowest, that is Saturn, the father of all the others.

That is why everything comes from the world of matter.

Our Hermetic School proceeds in its analysis from low to high, from *matter to light,* which is matter in the state of vibration; from *matter to magnetism,* which is the specific potential of its atomization; from *matter to trance,* which corresponds to the passive state of consciousness for the freeing of the divinity [*Nume*], which is intensification of Light.

So our organism has no parts beyond the anatomic divisions, but its components are *bodies* of an elementary and complex nature such that every atom, molecule, or cell specifically includes these *bodies* that are saturnian in their origin and, in their state of transformation, lunar and mercurial, evolving and sublimating, as far as the vibrating *body* of light, which is solar.*

The lunar body, conceived of as a fluid personality, of a lighter matter, which, containing the other two higher principles (solar and mercurial bodies) might separate from the physical body, would look like an angel/man (*angelus* = messenger) capable of moving without the need for a physical body.

The lunar body is the higher part of the material body, and the lower part of man's mentality or spirituality.

In the relationships of bodily life, the lunar body is used to receive the impressions of the outer and grosser body, and to express ourselves with a known word; it is formed of the least sensitive part of the intelligent nature and of the most delicate part of the physical body: it is the nervous channel or the channel of the very sensitive force in any animal organism. It is plastic and therefore capable of all possible forms.

It is most sensitive and consequently susceptible to the slightest fluctuations of will. Its plasticity, coupled with its very high degree of sensitivity, makes it changeable and makes it active as the receptacle of

*[Note from Hahajah, extract from the appendix of *Opera Omnia* by Giuliano Kremmerz, *La Scienza dei Magi,* vol. 3 (Rome: Edizioni Mediterranee). —*Ed.*]

all that acts sensibly upon it, and on it all sensory impressions stop and make their mark.

All the impressions of a sensorial origin pass from the saturnian body and constantly and continually reflect on the sidereal body, which is also called Christ (as *ichthys*) and the lamb of God on account of its meekness because, like the lamb, you can do what you will with the sidereal body.

Its plasticity, its sensitivity to impressions, is millions of times more delicate than the sensitivity of the most sensitive of photographic plates.

This accounts for, as we can accept without fear of error, all that asceticism attributes to it: "It is in you, it sees, feels, and remembers everything; it keeps everything for the day on which you shall be judged."

The sidereal body brings all the impressions of the senses together; it separates, mixes, and returns them on request, just as photographic negatives make copies of different sizes. It is the female of the physical body, that is, it receives from the physical body, through sensations, images of the physical world, keeps them, establishes them, nourishes them, and returns them, in an occult way, to the physical body that, forgetting that it created them, accepts them and becomes their envoy.*

The nervous system of the human organism (lunar matter) is the delicate intermediary between intelligence (mercurial matter) and the external world; by means of it, verbal, phonic, written, or drawn manifestations are possible. The whole essential part of man is found there, in the sensitivity of this lunar and pre-mercurial matter that constitutes our being. It is a filter of the influences of natural energies; it is a fine sieve that, selecting the impressions of external forces, brings them to the brain in a modified form.

Magical or Hermetic *purity,* but not religious purity, is the conscious and unalterable neutrality we keep compared with our fellow men. A man who, at the peak of his perceptive powers, can be *neutral,*

---

*[Note from Hahajah, extract from the appendix of *Opera Omnia* by Giuliano Kremmerz, *La Scienza dei Magi,* vol. 3 (Rome: Edizioni Mediterranee). —*Ed.*]

who can, therefore, keep his consciousness serene, integral, separated from sensations, and ready to judge them without any interest whatsoever, rises above the level of the human mob.

In the ordinary man, the pure intellectual principle (Sun) is enclosed in the mercurial body, which in its turn is contained in a lunar shell that is more corporeal and sensitive only to the volitive actions of the physical body; a common type who, not having developed his pure intelligence, bows before a god outside himself, that is, before voices, sounds, movements which the body apprehends outside and not within itself.

In profane society two gods are followed: the instinctive, individual god of one's base animality, and the one who speaks through other people's mouths, that is, in received ideas (scientific, religious, moral, and so on). What is silent in man living in society is simply the solar god, who, when he saw the alliance had been broken, hid his face.

An ordinary man is sensitive to a greater or lesser degree to sensory impressions from outside, that is to say, that he is at times more ready to reflect according to his constitution. The same man, on the same day, is in different conditions of physical consciousness. The state of perfect mastery of one's being is not constant in the same individual, whatever it may be. Notably, desire and the state of concupiscence breach the pure normality of consciousness and make it drowsy and go to sleep.

To strip oneself of the modernity of one's being is a very difficult thing to do; more for the cultured than for the uncultured, because the latter does not abound in fascinating and dazzling feelings, and older ways dominate in them more easily. The priestly purification imposed on the neophyte was just this cleansing of the consciousness of those aspiring to the light, the wiping away of any influence of the mob.

Only that one of pure consciousness is granted freedom beyond the relative limits of time and space, and my present comment wishes to indicate, as the only preparation, that this state of purified consciousness is the key to the Hermetic Gate.

Prayer, chastity, fasting, of which we have spoken, stripped of any mystical idea, contribute *to the gradual liberation of the lunar body, seat of the Magicians' astral, from the sensory impressions coming from the saturnian body. And this is not because the sensory impressions are no longer recorded as they arrive by the lunar body, but because their reception is no longer followed by an upsetting resonance in the affective and emotive spheres.*

With the conquest of such a state of freedom, our purified lunar body (the "Mary" of the Catholics) will no longer be the eternal battlefield between action and reaction, and only then will it be possible to begin to hear the "inner voice" that now speaks unheard in each of us.

The rites of purification have their raison d'etre in their effects. Initiation starts, in fact, not only in words, as soon as the vulgar man starts to hear the inner voice, the Christ, the angel, the genius.

•➤•

Now the chapter of Ariel is drawing to a close, and the only way I can sum up what I have said or hinted at about occult Ariel is to sum up the laws that allow you to come into the possession of the force in magic, laws that can be applied to the magical education of the disciple.

THE CATECHISM OF
THE FIRST STAGES OF MAGIC

Those who want to succeed must keep silent, but must operate while keeping silent.

To operate is to act.

You act on apparently inanimate things and on visible and invisible animate beings by means of three factors:

1. Will
2. Science
3. Equilibrium

1. RITES AND WILL

The rites are, for the disciple, like magical instruments, the key to any magic that develops; therefore, the rites against which all ignorant people rebel are the most powerful aids to educate and direct the will, to take the place of science in those who have none, to generate equilibrium in those who are subject to passions.

Whole religious stories are kept alive by rites full of wisdom, the key to which often—too often—is lost to the priests. If you abolish rites in this state of priestly consciousness, you will destroy religion.

A rite and a ritual formula do not magically obey the conscious personality of the operator; they obey the private consciousness of the individual, that is, the occult consciousness of the integral individual.

If there is no homogeneity between the occult and normal consciousness, the effect of the rite, although it is a definite contribution to the chain of the Schola,* is often in direct contradiction to the desires expressed by the practitioner.

In magic the practice of a rite is, in itself, an arcanum because he who enacts it must will, and in magic the Hermetic meaning of the word *will* is not what we humanly understand it to be.

Hence many misinterpretations, much dejection, a great many mistakes. Human exercise of will lies in the specific mastery of the impulsive passion that often takes the form of logical reasoning; so it seems that when we humanly will something, we will it with our whole selves, whereas it is only the relative, lower consciousness that has become intoxicated.

Will has a real magical potential either when it is the predominating expression of our occult consciousness or when the outer personality agrees with the occult individual within us.

In those who act magically, we can notice the same as can be noticed in mediums. In them the state of trance, when it is deep, often shows an occult personality in direct contradiction with the visible one.

---

*[Presumably Kremmerz refers here to a Hermetic school or order. —*Ed.*]

The integration of man begins when his conscious personality coincides with the consciousness of the occult and historical man.

Those who do not understand this must not waste their time trying to perform magic, because they are destined to fail.

A magical practice differs from religious prayer in that the former must found its volitive power on the inner will and enhance the worth of the image (*imago* = *in-magus*); while the latter comes from the exterior consciousness that believes in what is above and in what it does not see.

To educate the will is to direct it; to replace science is to generate: active equilibrium cannot be obtained without the magical method.

Regnum regnare docet [the kingdom teaches to rule]: to operate is to learn while acting. You go to the war first as a conscript and then as a veteran, but when you are a veteran you can show the wounds received when you were a conscript.

2. WILL AND DESIRE

In order to initiate oneself into the practice of magic, one must determine clearly one's will and its purpose.

Willing and knowing how to will is a great secret.

Those who will and do not know how to will are not magicians and will never become such.

To will is not to desire. Desire kills will. Desire without will is enough to destroy any work of magic.

3. WILL AND INVOCATION

The angel of the will is *Ariel,* strength or will, because the most powerful force is the will of a man who knows what he wants.

Without repeating myself, I say to my disciples: if you want to draw strength to yourself, invoke and evoke *Ariel,* and the angel will bring it to you.

To *invoke* means to call in oneself.

To *evoke* means to call to oneself.

All things that are called will come. Orpheus moved mountains playing his lyre.

One must become like a little Orpheus to draw toward oneself the invisible atoms of the generating force which is Universal Life.

4. ARIEL AND THE WILL-SOUL

This universal life consists of tangible and ethereal matter. But ether is matter also; consequently, life is matter. The vibrating action of this matter is intelligence in motion, or active will, which as a resulting outcome of matter in vibration is matter-soul.

Ariel, like all angels, like all spirits, like everything that is, must be considered tangible in every respect, even in the ultra-normal intuitions of the human mentality.

Invoke Ariel if you want to become strong.

Ariel comes when the weak call him to help them in all good works.

David stands before Goliath. Jehovah sends him Ariel. The stone hits the giant; but the cause was just in the integral concept of the Israelite phase, otherwise Ariel would not have answered, or he would have become a devil and cheated the daring boy.

All this means that Ariel lends his strength only to *just* men. He only helps *just* causes.

Therefore, to invoke the god of force one must feel, or better, identify oneself with divine justice.

By this I wish to warn those who think they can use visible or invisible spirits only to satiate filthy lust. In order to draw the angels one must be have the justice of God, otherwise winged spirits, like the eagle, will not come. I have said and repeated this many times.

In invocations, human nature coincides with a nature similar to its own, on a different level. When such a nature is a god, the operator is deified.

5. WILL AND WORDS

There are rites and conjurations for successful *invocations*. The Latins called them *carmina,* the Hebrews called them *psalms,* the Italians, *spells.*

The vibrations that set the ether in motion in the world of very fine matter are rhythmic by their very nature.

Sublime mathematics contains the keys to the series and relationships between the vibrations generated by will and the repercussion of the volitive act of ether on the tangible and visible world.

Words are articulations of musical notes produced from the mouth, a kind of trumpet whose sound is modulated at will. Each note corresponding to a syllable or a letter has a vibrating value on the ether. The arts of oratory and drama and singing are based on the theory of sounds, except when the harmony of ideas does not coincide with the art. Words act tangibly, like all sounds, on the auditory apparatus of sensitive persons.

But that is not all.

Certain sounds produced in a particular way act powerfully on the human psyche as a magnet does on iron. The experiments of sounds on sleepwalkers who fall into catalepsy are old. In the theater huge crowds of spectators are drawn by a note produced by a sweet and powerful voice. In an army and before a battle a few words spoken by a leader can decide the outcome.

Therefore, the word or rhythmic sound has a powerful and tangible effect on living things. The grandmother's lullaby sends the child in his cradle to sleep, the child who has not yet become conscious of ancient ideas carried on from his previous lives, and on whom the singing acts mechanically.

Therefore, the word is a force.

Ariel is or can be invoked by means of powerful words.

6. WILL AND CONJURATIONS

These powerful words are songs and articulated emissions of will.

Whether they be animated or not by concrete ideas, these words are the more powerful the more magnetism they have imbued in them by other operators, and the more their sounds correspond to the ideas you want to awaken.

The psalms of the Hebrews are magical. But in Hebrew they have more power than in Latin, and you must have the key to use them; but more powerful than the psalms are the imprecations, exorcisms, and spells of Egyptian and Chaldean magic because when they are pronounced or sung not only are the ideas of the previous generations in the astral zone awakened, but the spirits of fifty and more centuries of practitioners who have mechanically repeated them are involved in giving them force.

That is why these spells are given only to those who deserve them, because they are forces by themselves already actively vitalized, so much so that their effects are rapid and precise, unlike prayers already accepted in Catholic liturgy (the psalms) which have a relative value on account of the different manner in which they have been used.

If a magician tells you that with one word he put thieves to flight, believe him, because it is possible. If a practitioner of devilish magic tells you that he possessed a woman just by speaking to her for the first time, believe him, because it is possible.

Certain words, which we do not repeat in vain, are the patrimony of very exceptional men who will spoil their effectiveness if they overuse them, because they learned these words directly from the heaven of Ea, and each of them contains in synthesis an embryonic act of creation. Woe betide those who do not utter words in time, thus allowing the vital germ of creation to miscarry!

The invocations of the usual rituals and grimoires are almost worthless. The spells are not spoken when people can hear them with the ears of the physical body, but are shot like so many arrows, at a distance or close at hand, at the mental body of things or of beings that are evoked.

In magic *not to speak* means also not to say useless words.

When the magician speaks, he must operate.

When you speak, you heal, console, save, or kill.

The mystery of words and sounds in magic is a deep one.

7. WILL AND GRAPHIC SIGNS

We must now consider additionally that each word is not only a sound but also a graphic expression of the sound, if the vibratory waves of the sound are reflected on the delicate devices that serve as receivers. I have given the example elsewhere of the sensitive phonogram from a phonograph where the sound is spontaneously recorded. Considering that the nature of the human psyche is a thousand times more sensitive that a phonogram, you can understand that each sound can be translated into graphic signs. So Ariel is in the expression of signs: when the signs are graphic and are generators of force, the angel comes at your mere drawing of these characters.

To explain more clearly.

The disciple in magic must not only study deeply the value of words articulated in time to generate sensations, but he must also translate them graphically by means of the *sphygmic* art or *art of pulsations* and of beats, whose general and some particular laws are found in that well of truth that is the Hebrew Bible, written in Hebrew letters without dots, and for those who do not know Hebrew, in Plato, Aristotle, and Avicenna; and for those who know only the vernacular, certain traces, very few indeed, can be found in the poets before Dante Alighieri, in Dante himself, and in Petrarch.

Between the thought and the character representing it there is a whole law of evocation and reproduction of the labor involved in generating it.

Ciphers, characters, sacred words, have a value corresponding not to the will of those who use them for the first time but to the sum of all the wills of those who used them, namely, millions of strong, serene, and effective wills.

Talismans represent creations of the initial wills or evoked will, something like a psychical tool, that is, one that acts on the psyche or soul by impressing like a seal on the virgin wax of the soul the subtle properties evoked through signs, ciphers, and so forth.

Their power depends on the relative perfection and force of the one who makes and keeps them; and their effects come more or less speedily and are more or less powerful depending on the ciphers, characters, analogies and the magical capacity of the one who makes them.

They are analogical manifestations of will and not of desire.

They are reflected manifestations of will on the human soul, instruments of little, brief miracles of time, of force, and of expansion limited to willed effects, according to the intensity of the force of the one who has made them.

8. SCIENCE AND WILL

Ariel-force is the principle and consequence of *science.* Science is the intensive and concrete application of force in magic. The magus must have a perfect knowledge of the action of psychical and hyperphysical forces in order to obtain the realization of Ariel.

By this it is proved that in magic no application, explication, or adaptation of will exists without the foreknowledge of the way it works. Those who act on impulse by the revelation from that sensitive subconscious, which forms the substrate of mediums and hysterics, are not magicians but good subjects in the hands of a person who knows what he does and how to do it. On the contrary, those who consciously work, even if only employing a very small portion of their will-force, can be called magicians or sages.

I will digress for a moment to say *why* therapy classifies the most presumptuous physicians among the empirical. All the abovementioned scientists, including the physicians who diagnose known infirmities, are infallibly such when they do not depart from the observation of the immutable laws of nature in matter, in the order of creation, in the *spirit,* and in the natural and inferior elements.

The physician appears out of the darkness of old empirical medicine, studying the human body assiduously until he can describe the minutiae invisible to the naked eye. Cast a glance at the history of anatomy, up to the improved microscope, and you will see that man has wanted to realize exactly what the human body is made up of. He has succeeded. There is no cell that has not been explained by research. There is no pore that is not the subject of a specialized text. But when man has wanted to give health to his infirm body, his science has failed him, and the tombs opened and open today as in the time of Irnerius and the School of Salerno!

The pathogenic elements that contemporary physicians look for in bacteria to explain the spread of diseases and that will go out of fashion faster than we think, will be found by future medicine in an element inconceivable to present-day research: in the spirit of man in contact or in contrast with the spirit of things. Then a deep revolution in human knowledge will take place and that will mark the end of the world—that is, the end of the world of educated ignorance that hurls thunderbolts and excommunications against those who contradict it. The age of darkness will come to an end, and a new era will begin in which human sciences will be sciences of the human spirit. Then the social condition of peoples will change, because the spirit of Christ will have become flesh; human justice will be a precise, conscious, and constant reflection of *divine justice* that today, to imperfect man, often seems like divine injustice because men, who are *relative* in all their conceptions, can neither imagine nor understand justice in the *absolute.*

To study the vital principle in us, to separate it if it is separable, to integrate it if it is integrable, to bring it to the peak of its potentiality, to make it capable of drawing the maximum energy from the source of the universal life-principle, until it can use it and nourish itself on it, and nourish the organisms which lack it: all this represents the

Hermetic education and leads to the concept of a *Hermetic physician*. Hermeticism finds a help, which all modern physicians fail to consider, in the spirit or deep intelligent vitality of the patient, on which spirit you cannot act with drugs but with the quintessence of all the drugs of the three kingdoms, which is synthesized in the *spirit* or intelligent vitality of the physician who cures, that is, helps the patient to overcome his illness.

The arcanum of the recovery of strength is, in its mechanics of self-nutrition, conceivable because it explains the result of the revivification of human strength after a very short and light sleep, but it cannot be proved by the ordinary methods of scientific demonstration.

No vitalist theory has ever come near the conception of a man's synthetic vitality being connected to a center, a nodule, or magnetic cell making up the being and that is in a relationship of reverberation and resupply with a terrestrial magnetic center that, in turn, is connected to the magnetic center of the planetary and stellar worlds of the whole universe.

Single center of energy: single magnetism.

Not unity of force, but a single central force of life, all expressions of which are only states of being.

The essential intelligence of the being, which is a predominant part of distribution, causes adaptations and rapidly changing forms of the specific units.

Sleep is the indispensable condition to restore our used energies. All the dispersions of our energy are accumulated currents of vital magnetism that are externalized and enter into the great invisible river of terrestrial and universal vibrations to return to the universal center of life.

If the integration of human powers can lead to the formation of the magus, a living reservoir of forces drawn from richer sources of energy, a simple progression of the magnetic richness accumulated in us through a provocation of acts and attractions of nonhuman entities can make divine or Hermetic medicine possible so that we can be useful to all those who suffer and come to us.

Knowing that we are radiating centers of life, drawing intelligent and essential vitality from the inexhaustible center of the universe-world, allows us to conceive the value of the Lord of causes as being the most bountiful, measureless, and the noblest provider ever conceived by religious or mystical imagination.

In patients, every crisis that heals takes place in sleep; a pain disappears only in sleep; the state of coma is a state of sleep in which the magnetic nuclear centers strive to secure a resupply that does not come, and when the means that make up the human organism as a center of magnetism become too weak, the dissolution of the organism is at hand.

To return to the point: as in profane knowledge, empiricism is excluded and cursed because only the application of what we know is considered wise; in the high sciences of the spirit only a man who uses the spiritual laws conscientiously can be called a magus, *cum scientia et ratione* [with science and reason], as the Scholastics used to say.

Where science is, Ariel is, that is, the divine and magical force, capable of working miracles; because as the visible world is known to the profane, so the invisible must be known to the initiate. Who are you, in following the inspiration without having the knowledge of the inspiration itself who can obtain an accidental result? Are you a magician or are you the plaything of the manifestation of the unknowable and the invisible?

9. HOW FORCE IS COMMUNICATED

If you have a visible master, beware that his science is a light that cannot be given away, but as fire kindles dead coals, by communicating the elementary Ariel of fire, he kindles in your soul the fire of science and through the science he communicates the force to you. The method wished for by the profane, of an exposition of the laws of knowledge to the disciple, cannot be followed and cannot be adapted to the teaching of magic.

To convert you, if you are prepared for an improvement, the master calls upon your developed reason and he affiliates you to his school to make your first steps easy. Like a master to the pupils in the common school, he gives you what he thinks is useful.

But, says the sceptic, what can convert us is the imposing result. If you pretend to be a master and want to convert us, do so.

But what does the master care if you do not want to convert yourself to spirituality?

The question resembles that of a child who was visiting Saint Peter's:

—Daddy, why don't you buy a dome like Saint Peter's to put on our house?

The father, smiling, said to his son:

—Dear child, our house is not fit for that dome; we must first prepare the house, then we will put the dome on it.

Do you think, you who have a sound intellect, that the organism of a spiritually evolved man, capable of giving you proof of transcendental and intellectual phenomena, can be the dome for any modest house?

I will simply tell you this: allow me to give you the certainty of an occult power, be it human or extra-human, through a progressive initiation. This practice serves to trim the naked psychical organism of the neophyte, giving him the possibility of achieving phenomena of a superior order, and it is the key to a whole philosophical building, which will have its great influence on the creation of a school that will facilitate individual research and the progress of those who will feel spurred on by success to continue their research.

Just as the superior intelligent world manifests itself to the inferior only through symbols, analogies, and assonant words, so the teaching of magic is accomplished through analogical acts, which the master practices upon the disciple.

The science of the masters of fire can be communicated only through contact, whereas the masters of light communicate it only in silence. When you read the holy books, says the Church, look at the spirit that is contained in them, but when you read the books of magic you must stop neither at the words nor at the spirit of words: *beyond what is said and shown there is a master who indicates a goal for you to reach, and stimulating the thirst of the disciple teaches, without saying so openly, how to reach the goal;* so to learn is to understand and to understand is to steal the force that nobody gives away to you: so in you the beast dies and the angel is born.

Magic is an aristocratic science and avoids teaching to the masses, which must have the intuition of the existence of the divine science, but cannot possess it. However, he who from the masses harvests the seed and conquers science and force, becomes monarch of all.

Know how to understand, and you will learn.

10. SCIENCE, WILL, AND FORCE

If you unite science and will, you will find the solution to the problem of force, but not the means to adapt and focus force on the things to be changed. But if science is in union with will transformed into force, all miracles are possible. Follow these rules to adapt the force:

1. Will without desiring
2. Will without fear
3. Will without regret

Wish, fear, and regret kill the will: before operating in difficult or doubtful things, do not start if you have not put a distance between yourself and the three sins of the magician.

If you desire, fear, and regret it, enchantment will not work, and all forces weaken.

In section two above I said that to will is not to desire; now I say that regret or fear neutralizes every act of will.

In order not to wish, not to fear, and not to regret, you must feel just in a divine way, that is, without the human prejudices of selfish justice.

11. EQUILIBRIUM AND FORCE

To inspire oneself by absolute justice means to be in equilibrium, to be just.

Therefore, will, science, and equilibrium are the three essential conditions of Ariel or the magus of force.

12. JUSTICE AND FORCE

Will without science and science without equilibrium is the negation of any kind of magic.

A magician must not do all he wants: only what it is right to do, otherwise his action would be a sinful violence against all power and all natures inferior to his own.

Do you want to have the force of a god? Be as just as a god! Do you want to have the force of a devil? Be as unjust as Satan!

Force in magic is a providential action that is fruitful and beneficial when it agrees with the providential principle; but it is not such when, by reaction, it draws against itself all the repercussions of justice done.

Reason is order; order is God, because order is justice.

Madness is disorder; disorder is Satan, because disorder is injustice.

13. PURITY AND FORCE

The magic of passions is dominated by invoking the purest Ariel. Passions are dominated through purity.

Pure force is without passion.

Impure force is rich in all the torments of passions. Magical and Hermetic purity is not religious purity. Our purity here, understood integrally, is the conscious and inalterable neutrality that we maintain toward our fellow men.

Purification means to eliminate all that modern education has imposed on us and present oneself naked for baptism—*sicut erat in principio* [as it was in the beginning]—thus unveiling the dormant self and evoking all natural powers of the soul in its simplicity.

Every feeling of hatred or love, every interest of the Hermetic operator in the realization of something desired, nullifies, destroys, and makes the expected result useless.

That is why I said that the feeling of *justice* is the only factor of any progress toward reintegration.

There is an obstacle, which opposes us, whenever our being moves toward evil.

Why does Hermetic medicine easily obtain miraculous results? Because you cannot come running to help the sick with hatred. Nobody can help or have the will to help a sick person he hates: it would be a contradiction of the aim of the work.

14. PASSIONS AND FORCE

Can passions be used as stimulants of the organism for the production and invocation of armed Ariel? I mean, can sin or vice be the stimulant for the unleashing of occult powers in some creatures?

Yes, but this is the despicable method of the sects of bad magicians. Divine magic finds a stimulus only in virtue.

Virtue is Ariel, virtue is force, virtue is purification. The pure source of divine magic lies in love of one's fellow men, in the sacrifice of oneself to one's fellow men, in the sacrifice of one's possessions to the redemption of others.

The love of one's fellow men must be Christian, that is, extremely pure, extremely chaste, and without any expectation of reward.

Sacrifice means pain.

In the deep poetry of love without expectation of reward and of pain without expectation of relief, pure magic finds the spring of all great miracles: the faith in the endless glory of the other world and the joy of coming near, through the burnt offering of one's own self, to Ea.

15. THE PURITY OF ARIEL

Good and evil in magic depend on the purity and justice of the operator rather than on the means the operator uses.

Good and evil must stay in the vestibule and not come into the temple; in the peristyle, that is, where the crowd of traders throng whom Christ drove out of the temple with his whip; but in the occult, where only the *inexorable law* of progress in nature and its generation exists, there can be only absolute good, that is, the *justice* that is Jehovah, the invisible god who manifests himself through his uncompromising and fatal goodness in the act of creation.

16. ARIEL THE CREATOR

The man who wants to achieve the power of working with the force, justice, and purity of Ariel must not in the generative acts of creation resemble men, nor must he model himself on their passions; in this lies his absolute resemblance to God, in this lies the complete success of his ascent, whatever his background, his means, his systems of creation and fulfillment. Devilish magic and angelic magic, white and black magic, are only vague and vain words before which there is only one fact: the possibility of the magician to imitate and penetrate divine nature, that is, the nature of things that can be and are to be created.

My disciple must learn that in order to give up all man's passions, to purify himself of all the grave and heavy chains that bind the body of the enshrouded angel, only two divine virtues have to be followed: *the love of men and forgiveness;* these two virtues are implied in the ideal of *charity.*

Man makes for himself a curious statuette of charity as he does of God, and nourishes it with ambition, vainglory, ignorance, human providence, and philanthropy. Let the sensible reader closely examine the institutions of civilization so that he may see how different they are from the divine charity of which Buddha and Christ speak. This marks how barbaric we are now, in an age when social selfishness predominates in all acts of the sovereignty of states as against the interests of the subjects. All the theories, which now seem the most utopian and impossible, would find their possible realization in the transformation of human nature into good, that is, in the divine regeneration of man fallen from his divine rights. But the law that governs spirits and things in their transformation is one: it is the *serial* law, geometric or arithmetical according to the value of progressions; it is a law of regeneration for suffering according to the degree of convulsion of the social organism. But *charity* is still very far from the modern ideal of trading charity in politics, in religious societies, and in families where gold, which represents the synthesis of all well-being, only serves to spread the prejudice that good lies in pleasure and evil in pain.* Human institutions have substituted the word *philanthropy* for the word *charity,* but only when philanthropy becomes charity again will we have gone up another step in priestly perfection.

Any disciple who works in magic must know how to love and forgive. Love without selfishness is divine, although women cannot conceive how they can be loved intensely and ideally without any blemish of jealousy, which represents the condensation of selfishness in love. Love is the most fascinating charity of instinct; its decadence is the prostitution of all noble feelings, that is, divine and divinizing feelings in men. Love is the most precious complement of social intercourse, and it is the key of the purest Isis that opens the fruitful treasures of divinity in fallen human creatures. The mysteries of Venus were nothing but the celebration of the cult of this comprehensive love, which unites the two poles of creation, in the creation of vital and intelligent Mercury. The Mystic Rose is the Rose of Love. *Le Roman de la Rose* and courtly love in the Middle Ages, the songs of the troubadours, the poems like Dante Alighieri's, Brunetto Latini's, and others are only the romances of charity in love, and the "romance" is *love through charity*. Nobody was ever

---

*According to these people, Mary, Our Lady of Sorrows, should be the evil Mary.

a poet without love; poetry is depicted as love; but in love there is truth, that is, charity in embryo. From here come the satanic rituals extolling the glory of generation made of impure love, abortion made of prostitution, and of life without love, of life that is entirely sensual and libertine.

Forgiveness is one side of the purest love. To know how to love means to know how to forgive. A father and mother forgive their son, who is their love. Among all false loves, the least false is motherly love because it is the least selfish. And yet not even motherly love is true, except in the unconsciousness of forgiveness, and the mother who cries over the pain, which regenerates her son, is selfish, as the great majority of mothers are.

Learn to forgive and you will become gods on earth. Let not the offense touch you, and consider your offender as an innocent child who spits in your face. Divine and divinizing magical education is education in forgiveness; otherwise a magician would become a powerful instrument against all the passions of other people.

Love and forgiveness united in *charity* are completely different from *philanthropy* on account of the divine character of the former and the human character of the latter. Charity is as powerful as the sacrifice of the relative being to the absolute being; *philanthropy* is the passion of zoophiles who try to protect animals, to alleviate their sufferings, but not to have them sitting at their dinner tables, nor to pull heavy carts in their stead.

Charity is the reaction of the world of matter against the world of spirit; *charity is* carnality spiritualized.

Christianity feels the charity of others, because it transforms itself into their flesh and physical sufferings, that is, it *feels the pain the others feel,* which is quite different from *philanthropy,* representing the pure and simple feeling of friendship toward a *suffering man.*

An example of charity is when the mother feels anguish in her gut when her child cries with hunger.

Philanthropy, on the contrary, is a cerebral virtue, which would not be afflicted by the show of other people's misery.

If every man evoked in himself the Christ who sacrifices himself for the good of other people, the society of present-day thieves would be changed into an earthly paradise. That is why it is said, *and I say,* that any character that causes separation is a social evil, and all good comes from human solidarity.

17. DOMINANT ARIEL

Those who succeed in changing hatred toward their enemies into love, dominate them inexorably. The triumph of love lies in the act of force of its justice and is unconquerable in its powerful victory.

Ariel as the force and attractive spirit of love is bountiful in forgiveness.

The virtues and vices of souls are exchanged in direct proportion to their reciprocal love, and in inverse proportion to their hatred. The stronger the love between two people, the more they exchange their respective virtues through their love.

This explains why you cannot dominate a person you hate, while you can possess the person you love.

This is the law by which the virtue of all real things is spread, and visible and invisible societies come together and break apart according to the same law.

Bismarck said that law was a silly invention of the weak, whereas there is no other law but force. In the absolute, he is right. This force is law because the god who is not just is not strong.

Remember the fable of the puppy who attacked a lion; the lion, bitten, found that the puppy's teeth had not even broken his skin. Then he said to his enemy: "Look, I could kill you and eat you. I will spare your life because you are so little." The puppy tried again, with the same result. The lion let him do it, and again spared him. Now, the force of the lion made him generous but, had the lion not been strong, he would not have had the forgiveness of the mighty.

Epilogue

O Ariel, ray and power of the force of Jupiter, after man, who is a microscopic part in the immensity of the universe, has known you, he sees the divine spark that was in him has been rekindled in its primitive splendor. Where are you? Do those who invoke you see you? Will those who invoke you hear you? What do you look like, O martial spirit, in blinding light and fire? What does your voice sound like in the harmony of visible things? What is your love like; what is your power?

In the Eastern civilizations you kindled the splendor and magnificence in Nineveh, Babylon, Memphis; in Thrace, Orpheus enchanted you; in Greece, Jason tried to conquer you, Hercules to charm you; in Rome, you became the eagle of knowledge and empire; in the Christian world, you spoke of the truth on the Cross.

In the world everybody invokes you, everyone adores you, because they only see of you the face of Amun, horned and bountiful; they do not know that you become providence through charity and that you are beneficent in the glory of justice.

Be bountiful in giving to my disciples, who call you in the high and silent hours of the night, as they burn the midnight oil in their studies where the volumes of human knowledge are accumulated. Appear to them in the form of a gnome or an elf, dazzling or ethereal, sitting on the frame of an ancient painting, then speak to the neophyte who wants to do and to know: tell him the truth, the naked truth; then smile upon him and give him time to reflect.

Among the things you will tell him, do not forget to address him thus:

There is no science without silence, no force without charity, no power without justice. I am the *virtue,* the one who transforms and makes miracles. I do not bind myself to you except in a pact, an alliance. You will tell me *I am yours, now and forever;* you will write with your own blood; you will put your imperfect soul into these drops of blood and you will wait; before accepting the pact, I will watch you closely. I will know if you have tried to sell me fake precious stones for sapphires; if the truth is in you, if your hope is your love, and . . . if all is truth, I will come to you. I will give you force in justice, love in charity, light in science. When you look for me, I will be near you; when you sleep I will watch over you; when you fight evil, I will be with you.

Let not the intelligent disciple, a neophyte in magic, be blinded by the spirit of the century; the guardian of the threshold whirls his enchanted blade. He strikes you with a flash from his powerful eyes, but the disciple will pass if he knows how to *keep silent, to will,* and *to love.*

Science is force, is justice, is charity. Science is not delirium, fever, passion, pride, ambition, lies. Lightning is an inexorable law, as is force in justice and as is charity.

In this science the martyrs of the great ideals found their smile in the face of death, and their happiness in the world of priestly empires.

Remember, my disciple, that you must be wise and must be able to *read* my words, because I have finished, and I am forbidden to tell you more because I have said too much, especially where you did not think I unveiled the arcanum of the magic of the great magicians as I had promised you.

The true initiate is the one who, after constant labors and an efficacious practice of the doctrine, made perfect and evolved, surpasses the highest steps of the visible vulgar world and enters the world of causes, giving up the world of effects.

It is the man who goes beyond the huge river of external sensations and feels developing within himself the inner man, that is, the speaking Christ.

It is the man who has separated himself, that is, he who has divided his "high body," his first trinity, from the contemporary body and mentality, moving into the phase of evolution from where he can no longer recede, and speaking the double language of the spirit and the man.

Since in every man there is, as it were, a double being—the ancient synthetic one of past lives and the modern new one—initiation must be understood as the return of the apparent man to the mysterious or arcane one.

Initiation begins with the work the master does on the disciple so that the ancient man manifests in his integrity.

Religions consist of spiritual education enveloping both the new and the ancient being in the same cloak of ideas, nourished by faith; initiation, on the contrary, prevents the formation of new layers around the occult and arcane being, and uncloaks him.

The continuous action of taking away the artificial to unveil the ancient spirit in its integrity is a continuous death of the artificial self, without the support of a moral aid or encouragement.

The novice must only instruct himself in science and aspire in silence to the manifestation of the God in himself without letting himself be seduced by the outer world.

The Jehovah of the disciple must manifest himself directly and immediately. The disciple proceeds through the development of intuitions and his liberation from all artifices.

He must not deprive himself of any desire to live, nor of any interest in earthly things, but he must aspire:

1. To the absolute mastery of life, as the creator of life itself.
2. To the possession of the state of holiness so that, according to the creative will that resides in him in the form of his highest solar principle, which itself is the prime virtue of the whole real

universe, he may make use of all material things, whether perceptible or not, considering them as his own production and not as goods that come to him or are donated by other hands, to make use of them according to the principle of absolute justice, the symbol of which is the scales of Michael.

3. To the possession of the state of mobility, so that all base things may be dominated.

4. To the reconquering of the luminous state, so that all roads, all principalities may be enlightened by truth; and so that he may always be conscious of himself, an active dominator, the creator and re-creator of things.

Magic with its operations expects only one phenomenon, one great phenomenon: that the sun rise, that the great god of mental light appears in the east of the sleeping psyche of the disciple, and that the day comes in the soul of the one who invokes it.

Now, those who want to study and practice magic must not forget that the knowledge of the inner self constitutes the first part of the intelligent and conscious manifestation of the disciple, after which one comes into relation with the world of causes, consciously and not by blind faith.

In Magic, as soon as the theoretical rudiments are learned, one must *operate*. To discuss is a waste of time; the disciple must *work, pray, practice*.

The practices of magic given by a master consistently have the following form: create, toil, experiment, and take no momentary notice of the psychical or soul work, which the operator takes no notice of simply because he does not immediately see what his operations produce; but the friendly hand he has invoked will begin, latently, to dispel the darkness and, unseen, insensibly, the labor of reintegration in the *beatifying light* will not be interrupted till the day of the complete triumph of the intellect of truth in him.

Only one phenomenon must you ask and expect of our doctrine:

the reintegration of your *intelligent self,* that your spirit be enlightened and may find the Light and, in light, the Master.

Once this unique and great phenomenon has happened, all the others are child's play: one knows what they are, and it will not be worth risking inebriation.

With this I have finished; I think I have written enough, that is, what suffices and is necessary to men of good will to achieve their aims.

Hail, O disciple, I greet you; remember the *clama, ne cesses* [cry, cease not] of Isaiah. The time is propitious.

Index

natural magic, 60, 70, 81, 140–41, 163
natural mediumship, 80
natural sensation, 84
Nature, 9
necromancy, 34
neophyte, 16, 122, 124, 125
nervous system, 191
neurasthenia, 75
novice, 122, 214

occult, the
  interest in, 1
  need for, 24
  propagandists for, 34
occult initiatory societies, 135
occultism, credo of, 107
occult sciences, 30
operations in magic
  ideal, 119
  periods of, 120–21
  prayer in, 119–20
  types of, 118

Papus, 28–29
parapsychology, 2–3
passions and force, 207
pentagram, 100
perception
  of action, 94
  projecting, with words, 58
  subtle, 92
Perfect Master, 65
peri-spirit, 31, 33, 36, 113
philanthropy, 209, 210
philosophical research, 127
physical heredity, 108
physiology, 84
Piccardi, Giorgio, x
planets, action of, 105

positiveness, 146
practice, 138, 139, 174–75, 182–83
practicing, 92, 158
prayer, 119–20
preparation, 43–59
pro salute populi (for the good of
  the people), 12
protogenerating unity, 93
psychic force, 31
psychophysical powers, study of,
  13
psychosomatic concept, xi–xii
public opinion, 45
purification, 206–7
purification substances, 72–73
purity
  of Ariel, 208–11
  color white and, 72
  elements of, 46
  force and, 206–7
Pythagorean, 17, 47–48, 140, 143,
  154, 169

reaction, 94, 120
reason, 37
reasoned faith, vii
redemption, work of, 124–25
reincarnations, 31
religion
  evolution of, 97
  magic and, 46–47
  science and, 8, 94–99
repercussions, 57
research
  esoteric, ix–xi
  initiatic, x–xi
  philosophical, 127
  scientific, viii–xi, x–xi
rites, 194–95

BOOKS OF RELATED INTEREST

Introduction to Magic, Volume I
Rituals and Practical Techniques for the Magus
by Julius Evola and the UR Group

Introduction to Magic, Volume II
The Path of Initiatic Wisdom
by Julius Evola and the UR Group
Translated by Joscelyn Godwin
Foreword by Hans Thomas Hakl

Revolt Against the Modern World
Politics, Religion, and Social Order in the Kali Yuga
by Julius Evola

Ride the Tiger
A Survival Manual for the Aristocrats of the Soul
by Julius Evola
Translated by Joscelyn Godwin and Constance Fontana

Men Among the Ruins
Post-War Reflections of a Radical Traditionalist
by Julius Evola

The Hermetic Tradition
Symbols and Teachings of the Royal Art
by Julius Evola

The Doctrine of Awakening
The Attainment of Self-Mastery According to the Earliest Buddhist Texts
by Julius Evola

The Yoga of Power
Tantra, Shakti, and the Secret Way
by Julius Evola

INNER TRADITIONS • BEAR & COMPANY
P.O. Box 388 • Rochester, VT 05767
1-800-246-8648 • www.InnerTraditions.com

Or contact your local bookseller